KitchenAid

BAKING BASICS

Techniques for Perfect Baking

pil

Publications
International, Ltd.

Pictured on the front cover (from top): Lemon Meringue
Pie (page 122) and Sunshine Chiffon Cake (page 44).
Pictured on the back cover: Meyer Lemon Bars (page 20).

ISBN-13: 978-1-4508-0049-5
ISBN-10: 1-4508-0049-1

Library of Congress Control Number: 2010925018

Manufactured in China.

8 7 6 5 4 3 2 1

Microwave Cooking: Microwave ovens vary in wattage. Use
the cooking times as guidelines and check for doneness before
adding more time.

CONTENTS

BAKING BASICS

Beautiful and delicious baked goods have one thing in common—a cook who knows good baking basics

SECRETS TO SUCCESS

- Read through the entire recipe and gather together the ingredients, kitchen equipment, and pans before beginning.
- Prepare certain ingredients ahead of time. Does your recipe call for toasted nuts or soften butter? Be sure to set the butter out or toast the nuts before you start measuring and mixing.
- Carefully follow each mixing step in the recipe. It is important not to over-mix or under-mix.
- Be sure to use the exact pan or dish called for in each recipe. Substituting a different sized pan will affect baking times.
- A kitchen timer will become your best friend: use one to help you keep track of mixing times and baking times.
- Don't crowd the oven, and try to avoid opening the oven door during baking so as not to alter the oven temperature.
- Set your baked goods on a wire rack away from the oven to cool.
- Adjust the oven racks. Oven racks may need to be set lower for cakes baked in tube pans.

- If two oven racks are used, arrange them so they divide the oven into thirds, then stagger the pans so they are not directly over each other.
- Preheat the oven about 15 minutes before beginning to bake.
- Place the baking pan or sheet on the center rack. If two or more pans are used, allow at least an inch of space between the pans and two inches between the pans and the walls of the oven for proper heat circulation.
- If the heat distribution in your oven is uneven, turn the baking pan or sheet halfway through the baking time.
- Filled pans should be placed in the oven immediately after the batter is mixed. Batter should not sit before baking because chemical leaveners begin working as soon as they are mixed with liquids.
- Avoid opening the oven during the first half of the baking time. The oven temperature must remain constant in order for a cake to rise properly.
- For even baking and browning of cookies, it is best to place only one baking sheet at a time in the center of the oven. However,

if you must bake more than one sheet of cookies at a time, rotate them from the top rack to the bottom rack halfway through the baking time.

- Most cookies bake quickly and should be watched carefully to avoid overbaking. Check them at the minimum baking time, then watch carefully to make sure they don't burn. It is generally better to slightly underbake rather than to overbake cookies.
- When reusing the same baking sheets for several batches of cookies, cool the sheets completely before placing more dough on them. Dough will soften and begin to spread on a hot baking sheet.

MEASURING TOOLS & TECHNIQUES

One of the foremost keys to successful baking is properly measuring ingredients. Unlike cooking, baking requires precise accuracy, and the first step to mastering such accuracy is using the proper tools. Novice bakers might not know that you should use different tools for wet and dry ingredients. Here are a couple handy tips:

- Wet ingredients such as milk, oil, water, and honey call for a liquid measuring cup. This type of cup is usually clear glass or plastic and has a spout and a handle. These measuring cups are available in a variety of sizes, and it is best to have both a larger one (8-cup) and a smaller one (1-cup).
- Dry ingredients such as flour, sugar, and baking soda call for a dry measuring cup. This type of cup is usually made from plastic or wood, comes in a set with a variety of sizes and has a handle. The dry measuring cup is designed so you that you can level off ingredients to get a precise measurement.
- Measuring spoons can be used for both wet and dry ingredients when the quantities are

small and range from ⅛ teaspoon up to 1 tablespoon. Do not substitute the teaspoons and tablespoons from your everyday flatware to measure ingredients.

To measure flour, first spoon it into a dry measuring cup until it is mounded over the rim, then level off the top with a straight-edged knife or spatula. Don't shake or tap the measuring cup or press the flour down; this compacts the flour and you may end up with too much, ultimately resulting in dry baked goods. If a recipe calls for "sifted flour," sift the flour before it is measured; if a recipe calls for "flour, sifted," measure the flour first and then sift.

Sugar is measured differently depending on the type of sugar you are using. For granulated sugar, simply dip the measuring cup into the container of sugar, then level off the excess as described above. Brown sugar must be packed down until it is level with the top of the measuring cup for an accurate measurement. To test if you've filled the cup properly, turn it upside down—if the sugar holds its shape, it's been correctly measured. Powdered sugar should be spooned into a measuring cup and leveled off like flour.

To measure liquid ingredients, place a liquid measuring cup on a flat surface and add the liquid until it reaches the correct amount. Make sure you read the measurement line at eye level; reading it from above looks different and will result in an inaccurate measurement.

It is easiest to measure thick, sticky syrups such as corn syrup, maple syrup, molasses and honey in dry measuring cups. Spray the measuring cup with nonstick cooking spray (or lightly grease it with vegetable oil) before measuring so the syrup will slide right out and not stick to the cup.

Stick butter and margarine have measurement markings right on the wrapper.

Be sure to look carefully at the markings before cutting the amount you need, because they are not always positioned correctly—sometimes the start of the markings is not aligned with the beginning of the stick. Vegetable shortening should be measured just like brown sugar, packed into a dry measuring cup (to eliminate any air pockets), then leveled off at the top with a straight-edged knife or spatula. Shortening is also sold in packages of 1-cup sticks, with measurement markings on the wrapper similar to butter. Vegetable oil should be measured in liquid measuring cups.

PREPARING PANS

- Grease baking pans and sheets only if directed to do so in the recipe. It is generally best to use vegetable shortening or nonstick vegetable spray to grease pans because butter and margarine can cause overbrowning at high oven temperatures. When baking pans are greased, the baked goods will have a softer surface. When baking pans are greased and floured, a slight crust will form which helps a tender baked item release from the pan.

- When baking cookies, avoid overgreasing; this will cause the bottoms to overbrown and the cookies to spread too much. Nonstick cookie sheets should never be greased, even if the recipe calls for greasing, as this can also cause cookies to spread too much.

- To grease baking pans or sheets, use a paper towel, waxed paper, or your fingers to apply a thin, even layer of shortening, or spray lightly with nonstick cooking spray.

- To grease and flour baking pans or sheets, grease as directed above, then sprinkle flour into the greased pan. Shake the pan to coat evenly with flour, then tap to remove excess.

- To line pans with waxed paper or parchment paper, trace the bottom of the pan onto a piece of waxed or parchment paper and cut it to fit. Grease the pan, but do not flour it. Press the paper onto the bottom of the greased pan. Parchment paper is not recommended for square and rectangular baking pans; however, aluminum foil does an excellent job of keeping pans clean and making bars easy to remove. A quick and easy way to line a baking pan with foil is to invert the pan and shape the foil over the bottom. Lift the shaped foil off and fit it into the upright pan. Make sure there is at least a 2-inch overhang of foil on each side to use as handles for lifting out the bar cookies after baking. If the recipe calls for a greased baking pan, the foil should be greased (which can be done easily with nonstick cooking spray).

COOLING

- Immediately remove yeast bread from the baking pan or sheet and place it on a wire rack to cool completely. Allowing the bread to cool in the pan will result in a soggy bottom.

- Crisps, cobblers, pies, tarts, bar cookies, and brownies can be cooled completely in the baking pan on a wire rack.

- Cool cupcakes, muffins, and quick breads in the pan for about 10 to 15 minutes. Then remove them from the pan and let them cool completely on a wire rack.

- Most cakes can be removed from the pan after 10 to 15 minutes of cooling on a wire rack. Two important exceptions are angel food cakes and flourless cakes. Because they have a more delicate structure, they are cooled completely in the pan.

- Angel food cakes and some chiffon cakes are cooled in the pan upside down. An angel food cake pan has three metal feet on which the inverted pan stands for cooling. If you use a tube pan instead, invert the pan on a heatproof funnel or narrow-necked bottle.

- If a cake has cooled too long and will not come out of the pan easily, warm it in a 350°F oven for about 5 minutes. Then, carefully remove it from the pan and let it cool completely on a wire rack.

- Many cookies should be removed from the baking sheets immediately after baking and placed in a single layer on wire racks to cool.

- Fragile cookies may need to cool slightly (1 to 2 minutes) on the baking sheet before being removed to wire racks to cool completely. Follow the instructions given in the recipe.

STORING

- Once yeast bread has cooled completely, wrap it in plastic wrap or place it in an airtight plastic food storage bag. Store the bread at room temperature; placing it in the refrigerator actually causes it to become stale faster. Breads containing milk and fat will last longer than those containing water and no fat.

- Store quick breads in plastic food storage bags or wrapped in plastic at room temperature for up to three days.

- Store one-layer cakes in their baking pans, tightly covered. Store two- or three-layer cakes in a cake-saver or under a large inverted bowl. If the cake has a fluffy or cooked frosting, insert a teaspoon handle under the edge of the cover to prevent an airtight seal and moisture buildup. Cakes with whipped cream frostings or cream fillings should be stored in the refrigerator.

- Meringue-topped pies are best when served the day they are made; refrigerate any leftovers. Refrigerate custard or cream pies immediately after cooling. Fruit pies can be covered and stored at room temperature overnight; refrigerate them for longer storage.

- Store soft and crisp cookies separately at room temperature to prevent changes in texture and flavor. Keep soft cookies in airtight containers. If they begin to dry out, add a piece of apple or bread to the container to help them retain moisture. Store crisp cookies in containers with loose-fitting lids to prevent moisture build-up. If they become soggy, heat undecorated cookies in a 300°F oven for 3 to 5 minutes to restore crispness. Store cookies with sticky glazes, fragile decorations, and icings in single layers between sheets of waxed paper.

- Bar cookies and brownies can be stored in their own baking pan, covered with aluminum foil or plastic wrap when cool.

DECORATING & GARNISHING

Sometimes all it takes is that one special finishing touch to make a dessert go from drab to dazzling. Here are some great ideas for dressing up your baked goods.

Cherry Flower: Cut a maraschino or candied cherry into six wedges, being careful to leave the bottom 1/3 of the cherry uncut. Gently pull out the wedges to make flower petals. Place a tiny piece of candied fruit in the center.

Chocolate Curls: Melt 7 (1-ounce) squares of chocolate; let cool slightly. Pour the melted chocolate onto a cold baking sheet and spread it out, about ¼ inch thick, into a 6×4-inch rectangle. Let the chocolate stand in a cool, dry place until set. (Do not refrigerate.) When the chocolate is just set, use a small metal pancake turner to form the curls. Hold the pancake turner at a 45° angle and scrape the chocolate into a curl. Use a toothpick or wooden skewer to transfer the curl to waxed paper. Store in a cool, dry place until ready to use.

Chocolate-Dipped Garnishes: Dip cookies, nuts, or fruit halfway into melted chocolate, then place them on waxed paper until the chocolate is set.

Chocolate Drizzle or Chocolate Shapes: For chocolate drizzle, place melted chocolate in a plastic food storage bag. Snip off a tiny piece of one corner; drizzle over the treat. For chocolate shapes, place a sheet of waxed paper onto an inverted baking sheet. Place melted chocolate in a plastic food storage bag and snip off a tiny piece of one corner. While gently squeezing the bag, guide the opening just above the waxed paper to pipe the chocolate in a steady flow, making the desired shapes. Stop squeezing and then lift the bag at the end of each shape. Let stand in a cool, dry place until the chocolate is set. (Do not refrigerate.) When set, carefully peel the shapes off the waxed paper. Store in a cool, dry place until ready to use.

Chocolate Shavings or Grated Chocolate: Create chocolate shavings by dragging a vegetable peeler across a square of chocolate in short quick strokes. For grated chocolate, working over waxed paper, rub chocolate across the rough surface of a grater, letting the pieces fall onto the waxed paper. The large or small holes of the grater can be used, depending on the size of the chocolate pieces you want.

Citrus Knots: Using a vegetable peeler, remove strips of peel from a lemon, lime, or orange. Place the strips on a cutting board. If necessary, scrape the cut sides of the peel with a paring knife to remove any white pith. Cut the strips into 3½×⅛-inch pieces. Tie each piece into a knot.

Citrus Twist: Diagonally cut a lemon, lime or orange into thin slices. Cut a slit through each slice just to the center. Holding each slice with both hands, twist the ends in opposite directions. Place the slices on a plate or the desired food to secure them.

Powdered Sugar or Cocoa Powder: Place the powdered sugar or cocoa powder in a small strainer and gently shake the strainer over the dessert. For fancier designs on cakes, brownies, or bar cookies, place a stencil, doily, or strips of paper over the top of the dessert before dusting it with sugar or cocoa. Carefully lift off the stencil, doily, or paper strips, holding firmly by the edges and pulling straight up.

Powdered Sugar Glazes: Combine 1 cup of sifted powdered sugar and 5 teaspoons of milk in a small bowl. Add ½ teaspoon of vanilla extract or another flavoring, if desired. Stir until smooth. If the glaze is too thin, add additional powdered sugar; if it is too thick, add additional milk, ½ teaspoon at a time. Use the glaze white or tint it with food coloring to fit any occasion.

Strawberry Fan: Place a strawberry on a cutting board with the pointed end facing you. Make four or five lengthwise cuts from just below the stem end of the strawberry to the pointed end. Fan the slices apart slightly, being careful to keep all of the slices attached to the cap.

Sugars, Sprinkles or Candies: Sprinkle cookies with coarse sugar, colored sugars or sprinkles before baking. Or, after baking, cakes and cookies can be frosted and then topped with colored sugar, sprinkles or candies. To decorate a cake, coat the side with sprinkles while the frosting is still soft.

Toasted Coconut or Nuts: Spread coconut or nuts in a thin layer on an ungreased cookie sheet. Bake in a preheated 325°F oven 7 to 10 minutes or until golden, stirring occasionally to promote even browning and prevent burning. Allow coconut and nuts to cool before using. Toasted nuts will darken and become crisper as they cool. To decorate a cake, sprinkle the side with toasted coconut or nuts while the frosting is still soft.

Tinted Coconut: Dilute a few drops of liquid food coloring with ½ teaspoon milk or water in a small bowl. Add 1 to 1⅓ cups

flaked coconut and toss with a fork until the coconut is evenly tinted.

GLOSSARY OF BAKING EQUIPMENT

SPATULAS

Spatulas, sometimes called scrapers, are flexible utensils with a paddle-like head attached to a handle. They come in a wide variety of sizes and are ideal for scraping out the insides of bowls, containers, and measuring cups. The larger ones are also good for blending dough and folding delicate mixtures together. You'll want a variety of sizes, shapes, and flexibilities based on your uses and preferences.

Wide flexible metal spatulas are a necessity for removing baked cookies from baking sheets.

These spatulas have a flat, square, or rectangular metal blade attached to a plastic or wooden handle. The spatula blade should be wide enough to slide under and pick up a whole cookie without having the cookie hang over the edges of the blade. The thinner the metal, the easier it is to slide under cookies without breaking or mangling them.

Long narrow metal spatulas have thin metal blades attached to plastic or wooden handles. They are useful for leveling off dry ingredients when measuring or loosening a baked and cooled cake from its pan, and are ideal for spreading batters and frostings. Some are 8 inches long and rigid whereas others are shorter and flexible. A flat spatula forms a straight line from handle to blade. An offset spatula is angled near the handle, causing the handle to be raised slightly.

WIRE WHISKS

Made of stainless steel wires that loop to form a bulbous shape, wire whisks are designed to aerate and mix. Larger balloon-type whisks are used for whipping air into ingredients such as egg whites and cream, while small and medium whisks are used for stirring hot  mixtures as they cook and blending ingredients together without beating a lot of air into the mixture. When purchasing whisks, choose those that have sturdy wires and handles that are easy to grip.

KNIVES

Good-quality knives are important in baking as well as cooking, but only a few of them are used with regularity. A chef's knife has a wide, slightly curved blade from 7 to 12 inches long; it is used for most chopping tasks (such as nuts, dried fruit, or chocolate) and for slicing rolls of dough. A paring knife has a short 2- to 3-inch-long blade and is used for peeling and slicing fruit, cutting out garnishes, and other small jobs. A long serrated knife is useful for cutting bread.

SIFTER

A flour sifter consists of a fine mesh screen and a mechanism to push flour through the mesh. Sifting aerates dry ingredients such as flour, powdered sugar, and cocoa powder; it also breaks up lumps and gives dry mixtures a uniform consistency. A sifter with a 2- to 3-cup capacity and a crank-type handle is a good choice, but a strainer can be used instead if you don't have a sifter. To clean, wipe with a damp paper towel or hand wash, but make sure the sifter is thoroughly dried.

GRATERS

A four-sided box grater is a versatile and inexpensive tool with several different size openings; it can be used for grating citrus peel and chocolate in addition to its more common functions of grating cheese and vegetables. Smaller graters with handles may be easier to use and more convenient for baking jobs— these can be kept in a drawer or hung on a hook with other utensils.

DOUBLE BOILER

A double boiler consists of two stacked pans. The top pan, which holds food, nestles in the bottom pan, which holds an inch or two of simmering water. 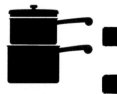 (The bottom of the top pan should never touch the water—it should only be warmed by the steam.) The purpose of a double boiler is to protect heat-sensitive foods like chocolate from direct heat. You can make your own double boiler by setting a stainless steel bowl over a pot of simmering water.

ROLLING PIN

Rolling pins are used to roll out dough for pies and cutout cookies. They can be made from hardwood, marble (which helps keep pastry dough cool), metal, plastic, or silicone (which provides a great nonstick surface). The typical American rolling pin is made of wood, has a handle on each end, and rolls on bearings; the French version has no handles. A heavy rolling pin allows for the most efficient rolling, because the weight of the pin does most of the work, requiring less effort from the user. Wood rolling pins should be wiped clean with a dry cloth (rather than washed) to prevent warping.

PASTRY BLENDER

This hand-held tool consists of several U-shaped wires or metal blades attached to a handle. It is used to cut butter or shortening into flour, which is an essential step in making pie dough. Two knives can also be used if you don't have a pastry blender on hand.

PASTRY BRUSHES

Pastry brushes are small, flat brushes made of natural bristles, such as boar bristles, nylon, or silicone. They are primarily used to apply melted butter or glazes to baked goods before or after baking, but they are also useful for brushing off excess flour from doughs and even for buttering the insides of baking pans. Brushes should be washed according to their specific instructions for washing, and then air-dried after reshaping the bristles. Nylon bristles tend to tear dough and may begin to melt when they come in contact with heat; boar bristle brushes are more expensive but last longer.

PASTRY BAG

A pastry bag (also called a decorating bag) is a cone-shaped bag made of canvas, plastic or plastic-lined cloth. It is used to pipe foods such as frosting, whipped cream, or dough in a decorative pattern. It is open at both ends. The food to be piped is placed in the larger opening, while the smaller opening is fitted with decorative tips made of plastic or metal. (A small, resealable plastic food storage bag with a tiny hole cut from the corner of the bag can also take the place of a pastry bag for simple decorating.) A quick alternative to a pastry bag for decorating baked goods is a plastic squeeze bottle—filled with melted chocolate or icing, it can make drizzling and decorating easier, especially for the novice.

PARCHMENT PAPER

Parchment is heavy paper that is impervious to grease and moisture. It is sold in sheets and rolls at gourmet kitchenware stores and at many supermarkets. When used to line baking sheets and pans, parchment paper provides a nonstick surface and allows for effortless removal of baked goods (and makes cleanup very easy). Parchment paper can also be made into cones that function as disposable pastry bags to pipe icing or chocolate.

OVEN THERMOMETER

Actual oven temperatures can sometimes vary quite a bit from the dial setting, so it is essential to keep a good-quality oven thermometer in your oven all the time and adjust the dial setting to compensate as necessary. If your oven temperature isn't correct, your baked goods will be underbaked or overbaked.

BAKING PANS

A baking pan is made of metal and has a square or rectangular shape with straight sides at least 1½ inches high. The most common sizes are 8 and 9 inches square; 11×7×2

inches; and 13×9×2 inches. Baking pans are designed for cakes and bar cookies. Shiny aluminum pans are ideal for producing a tender, lightly browned cake crust. Baking pans with dark finishes will absorb heat more quickly than shiny baking pans. When using baking pans with dark finishes or when substituting glass bakeware in recipes that call for baking pans, reduce the oven temperature by 25°F.

A baking sheet (often referred to as a cookie sheet) is a flat, rigid sheet of metal on which stiff dough is baked into cookies, rolls, biscuits, etc. It has a low lip on one or more sides for ease in handling; a lip higher than ½ inch interferes with surface browning, especially of cookies. The type of surface also determines the browning characteristics of the baking sheet. Shiny finishes promote even browning. Dark metal baking sheets absorb more heat and cause food to brown quickly. Insulated baking sheets have a layer of air sandwiched between two sheets of aluminum which helps to prevent excess browning but increases baking time. (Some cookie doughs may also spread more on these sheets.) Nonstick finishes minimize sticking and make cleanup easier. Baking sheets vary in size. Before buying, know the dimensions of your oven. A baking sheet should fit on an oven rack with at least one inch of space on all sides between the edge of the sheet and the oven wall. Otherwise, heat circulation will be hampered.

A bundt pan is a fluted tube pan traditionally used to bake a densely textured bundt cake. Bundt pans usually measure 10 inches in

diameter with a 12-cup capacity. They are traditionally made of cast aluminum with a nonstick interior coating, carbon steel with a nonstick finish, or lightweight aluminum. Generously greasing the fluted sides and center tube is extremely important to prevent sticking. Mini bundt pans are also available in several sizes (½-cup, ¾-cup, 1-cup, etc.) and shapes (straight, fluted, flowers, etc.). To make sure that the pan you are using is the size called for in the recipe, measure the amount of water that one bundt form will hold.

A cake pan, or layer pan, is a round baking pan with a straight side at least 1½ inches high. Pans made of aluminum or heavy-gauge steel will produce a cake with a delicate, tender crust. Besides the most common round 8- or 9-inch cake pans, there is a wide array of pans available that measure from 3 to 24 inches in diameter. Cake pans also come in a variety of specialty shapes.

A jelly-roll pan is a rectangular baking pan with 1-inch-high sides. It is used to make a thin sponge cake that can be spread with jelly and rolled into a jelly roll. Jelly-roll pans are also used for making thin sheet cakes or bar cookies. Standard pans measure 15½×10½×1 inches. They are available in aluminum and steel. Jelly-roll pans are not a good choice for baking individual cookies because the sides interfere with air circulation during baking, resulting in uneven browning.

Loaf pans are designed for baking yeast-bread loaves, quick-bread loaves, pound cakes, and fruit cakes. A standard loaf pan measures 9×5×3 inches with slightly flared sides. Smaller loaf pans measuring 8½×4½×2½ inches and miniature pans measuring 5×3×2 inches are also available.

Loaf pans come in a variety of materials including aluminum, steel, and glass. Loaf pans are also made in ceramic for oven-to-table presentations.

Muffin pans are rectangular baking pans with 6 or 12 cup-shaped cavities. A standard muffin cup measures 2½ inches in diameter and is 1½ inches deep. Also available are jumbo  muffin pans with cups measuring 3¼ inches in diameter and 2 inches deep, and mini muffin pans with cups measuring 1½ to 2 inches in diameter and ¾ inch deep. Muffin pans are made of aluminum, steel, cast iron, and a variety of other materials.

A pie pan or plate is exclusively designed for baking a pie. Pie plate generally refers to a glass or ceramic dish that can be used in the oven as well as on the table for serving. Pie pan generally refers to something made of metal. Both are round, about 1½ inches deep and have sloping sides. They range in diameter from 8 to 12 inches. Nine inches is the most popular size. Deep-dish pie pans are 2 inches deep. Glass or dark metal pie pans produce a crisp, golden brown crust. Shiny aluminum pans produce a paler crust.

A springform pan is a two-piece round baking pan with an expandable side (secured by a clamp or spring) and a removable bottom. When the clamp is opened, the rim expands and the bottom of the pan can be removed. This makes it easy to remove cheesecakes, cakes, and tortes from the pan. The diameter ranges from 6 to 12 inches, with 9- and 10-inch pans being the most common. Always check the size and volume capacity of your pan to be sure it's correct for the job.

A tube pan is a round baking pan with a hollow tube in the center, which conducts heat to the center of the cake to promote even baking. The tube also supports delicate batters as they rise in the oven. Most tube pans have high, slightly flared sides. Some, such as the angel food cake pan, have a removable bottom. They are generally 8 to 10 inches in diameter and 3½ to 4 inches high with a 12-cup capacity.

COOLING RACKS

A cooling rack is a raised wire rack used to cool baked goods. It is raised to allow air circulation around the baked goods or baking pan, which speeds cooling and prevents steam accumulation that results in soggy treats. Choose stable racks that are at least ½ inch high for good circulation, with the metal wires close together so very small or delicate cookies don't fall between them. Another option is a wire mesh rack (with small square grids) that provides more support and eliminates the problem of cookies slipping between the wires. Cooling racks come in various sizes and are available with a nonstick coating.

FOOD PROCESSORS

A food processor can be used for mixing doughs and batters. It also chops, slices, shreds, and purées in a fraction of the time it takes to do these tasks by hand. You should consult the manufacturer's directions for making dough in your food processor.

GLOSSARY OF BAKING TERMS

Beat: Beating is the technique of stirring or mixing vigorously. Beating introduces air into egg whites, egg yolks, and whipping cream; mixes two or more ingredients to form a homogeneous mixture; or makes a mixture smoother, lighter, and creamier. Beating can be done with a variety of tools, including a spoon, fork, wire whisk, rotary eggbeater, or electric hand or stand mixer.

Blanch: Blanching means cooking foods, most often vegetables, briefly in boiling water and then quickly cooling them in cold water. Food is blanched for one or more of the following reasons: to loosen and remove skin (tomatoes, peaches, almonds); to enhance color and reduce bitterness (raw vegetables for crudités); and to extend storage life (raw vegetables to be frozen).

Blend: Blending is the technique of mixing together two or more ingredients until they are thoroughly combined. The ingredients may be blended together with an electric hand or stand mixer or electric blender, or by hand using a wooden spoon or wire whisk.

Boil: To bring to a boil means to heat a liquid until bubbles break the surface. Boiling refers to cooking food in boiling water. For a "full rolling boil," bubbles break the surface continuously and cannot be stirred away.

Brush: Brushing refers to the technique of applying a liquid such as melted butter, barbecue sauce, or glaze to the surface of food prior to or during cooking with a brush. It serves the same purpose as basting: preserving moistness, adding flavor, and giving foods an attractive appearance.

Caramelize: Caramelizing is the technique of cooking sugar, sometimes with a small amount of water, to a very high temperature (between 310°F and 360°F) so that it melts into a clear brown liquid and develops a characteristic flavor. The color can vary from light golden brown to dark brown. Caramelized sugar, sometimes called "burnt sugar," is used in a variety of desserts and sauces.

Chill: Chilling is the technique of cooling foods, usually in the refrigerator or over ice, to a temperature of 35°F to 40°F. A recipe or dish may require several hours or as long as overnight to chill thoroughly. To chill a large portion of a hot mixture such as soup or chili, separate the mixture into several small containers for quicker cooling. To chill small amounts of hot food, place the food in a bowl or saucepan over a container of crushed ice or iced water, or chill the food in the freezer for 20 to 30 minutes.

Chop: Chopping is the technique of cutting food into small, irregularly shaped pieces. Although the term does not designate a specific size, most cooks would suggest that food be chopped into approximately ¼-inch pieces. Chopped food is larger than minced food and more irregularly cut than diced food. Recipe directions may call for a coarsely chopped or a finely chopped ingredient.

Coat: To coat means to cover food with an outer layer, usually fine or powdery, using ingredients such as flour, crumbs, cornmeal, or sugar. With foods such as chicken, fish fillets, and eggplant, this coating is preliminary to frying or baking and provides a crispy exterior. Such foods are often first rolled in eggs or milk so the coating adheres. Some cookies are coated with sugar before or after baking.

Combine: Combining is the process of mixing two or more liquid or dry ingredients together to make them a uniform mixture.

Core: Coring means to remove the center

seed-bearing structure of a fruit or vegetable. The most commonly cored foods are apples, pears, pineapple, zucchini, and cucumbers. First cutting the food into quarters and then cutting out the center core can accomplish coring with a small knife. A utensil specially designed to remove the core of specific whole fruits and vegetables is known as a corer.

Cream: Creaming is the process of softening sugar and butter until the mixture is light or pale in color and well blended. Creaming can be done with a variety of baking tools including a wooden spoon, or an electric hand or stand mixer.

Crimp: To crimp means to seal two layers of dough together. This process can be done with one's fingertips or a fork, and the term is most commonly used in reference to pie crusts. Depending upon the style of pie, crimping can be used as a decorative finish for ornate desserts.

Crumble: To crumble means to break food into small pieces of irregular size. It is usually done with the fingers. Ingredients often crumbled include blue cheese and bacon. Both foods can be purchased in the supermarket already crumbled.

Crush: Crushing means reducing a food, such as crackers, to small fine particles by rolling with a rolling pin or pounding with a mortar and pestle. A food processor or blender also works well. Fruit can be crushed to extract its juices. Garlic is sometimes crushed with the flat side of a knife blade or in a garlic press to release its flavor.

Cutting In: Cutting in is the technique used to combine a chilled solid fat such as shortening or butter with dry ingredients such as flour, so that the resulting mixture is in coarse, small pieces. A fork, two table knives, fingers, or a pastry blender may be used.

If using a food processor, be careful not to overmix the ingredients. This process is used to make biscuits, scones, pie pastry, and some cookies.

Deglaze: Deglazing is the technique used to retrieve the flavorful bits that adhere to a pan after a food, usually meat, has been browned and the excess fat has been drained. While the pan is still hot, a small amount of liquid (water, wine, or broth) is added and stirred to loosen the browned bits in the pan. The resulting liquid is used as a base for sauces and gravies.

Dice: To dice is to cut food into small cubes that are uniform in size. The smallest dice, which is about ⅛ of an inch, is best suited for delicate garnishing. More typical are sizes between ¼ and ½ of an inch. Dicing is distinguished from chopping and mincing by the care taken to achieve a uniform size for an attractive presentation.

Dot: This term, generally used in cooking as "to dot with butter," refers to cutting butter into small bits and scattering them over a food. This technique allows the butter to melt evenly. It also keeps the food moist, adds richness, and can promote browning.

Dust: Dusting is a technique used to lightly coat a food, before or after cooking, with a powdery ingredient such as flour or powdered sugar. The ingredient may be sprinkled on using your fingers or shaken from a small sieve or a container with holes on the top. A greased baking pan can be dusted with flour before it is filled, a technique also known as "flouring."

Flake: To flake refers to the technique of separating or breaking off small pieces or layers of a food using a utensil, such as a fork. For example, cooked fish fillets may be flaked for use in a salad or main dish.

Flour: To flour means to apply a light coating of flour to a food or piece of equipment. Applied to food, the flour dries the surface. This helps food brown better when frying and keeps food such as raisins from sticking together. Baking pans are floured for better release characteristics and to produce thin, crisp crusts. Rolling pins, biscuit cutters, cookie cutters, and work surfaces are floured to prevent doughs from sticking to them.

Fold: Folding is a specialized technique for combining two ingredients or mixtures, one of which usually has been aerated, such as whipped cream or egg whites. It is best done by placing the airy mixture on top of the other and, with a spatula, gently but quickly cutting through to the bottom and turning the ingredients over with a rolling motion. The bowl is rotated a quarter-turn each time and the process repeated until the mixtures are combined with as little loss in volume as possible. Care must be taken not to stir, beat, or overmix. Fruit pieces, chips, or nuts may be folded into an airy mixture using the same technique.

Glaze: To glaze a dessert means to add a type of icing or topping that will give the dessert a smooth or shiny finishing coat. There are a number of different types of glazes. Pastry glazes, which are brushed onto dough before baking, are often made of egg, milk, and cream. Caramel and sieved jam can also be used as glazes.

Grate: Grating refers to the technique of making very small particles from a firm food like carrots, lemon peel, or Parmesan cheese by rubbing it along a coarse surface with small, sharp protrusions, usually a metal kitchen grater. Food may also be grated in a food processor using a specialized metal blade.

Grease: To grease a pan means to coat the inside surface of a pan or dish with a layer of fat. Butter, oil, and shortening are the most popular ingredients used for greasing, but recipes will often specify which type of fat to use. Pans can be greased with a brush, paper towel, or plastic wrap

Knead: Kneading refers to the technique of manipulating bread dough in order to develop the protein in flour, called gluten, to ensure the structure of the finished product. Kneading also aids in combining the dough ingredients. Biscuit dough is lightly kneaded—only about ten times—whereas yeast doughs may be vigorously kneaded for several minutes.

Level: Leveling refers to the leveling of ingredients when measuring or removing the crown, or rounded part, of a cake to create a flat surface conducive to frosting or decorating. The best way to level a cake is with a sharp serrated knife or a tool called a cake leveler.

Mash: To mash is to crush a food into a soft, smooth mixture, as in mashed potatoes or bananas. It can be done with a tool called a potato masher or with an electric mixer. Small amounts of food, such as one or two bananas or a few hard-cooked egg yolks, can be mashed with a fork. For best results with potatoes, make sure they are fully cooked so they are soft enough to become smooth.

Purée: To purée means to mash or strain a soft or cooked food until it has a smooth consistency. This can be done with a food processor, sieve, blender, or food mill. For best results, the food must be naturally soft, such as raspberries or ripe pears, or cooked until it is completely tender. Puréed foods are used as sauces and as ingredients in other sweet or savory dishes. The term also refers to the foods that result from the process.

Proof: Proofing is the process by which dough expands and rises and is called for in all yeast bread recipes. Dough proofs when it sits in a warm spot, free from draft, for several hours. The dough rises during the proofing process because the yeast converts glucose and other carbohydrates to carbon dioxide gas.

Reduce: To reduce is to boil a liquid, usually a sauce, until its volume has been decreased through evaporation. This results in a more intense flavor and thicker consistency. Typically, reduced sauces are one third or one half of their original volume. Use a pan with a wide bottom to shorten preparation time. The reduced product is referred to as a "reduction." Since the flavor of any seasonings would also become concentrated when a sauce is reduced, add the seasonings to the sauce after it has been reduced.

Roll Out: To roll out means to flatten dough into an even layer using a rolling pin. To roll out pastry or cookie dough, place the dough—which should be in the shape of a disc—on a floured surface, such as a counter, pastry cloth, or a large cutting board. Lightly flour your hands and the rolling pin. Place the rolling pin across the center of the dough. With several light strokes, roll the rolling pin away from you toward the edge of the dough. Turn the dough a quarter-turn and roll again from the center to the edge. Repeat this process until the dough is the desired thickness. If the dough becomes sticky, dust it and the rolling pin with flour. If the dough sticks to the surface, gently fold back the edge of the dough and dust the surface underneath the dough with flour.

Scald: To scald means to heat some type of liquid, usually a dairy product such as cream, in a saucepan until it is almost boiling. Tiny bubbles around the perimeter of the pan are often a good indicator that the liquid has reached the scalding stage. Scalded milk is often essential to custards, pudding, and sauce recipes.

Sift: Sifting is the technique of passing a dry ingredient such as flour or powdered sugar through the fine mesh of a sieve or sifter for the purpose of breaking up lumps and making it lighter in texture. Sifting results in lighter baked goods and smoother frostings. Most all-purpose flour is presifted, but many bakers sift even presifted flour to achieve a fine, light texture. Cake flour is generally sifted before using.

Simmer: To simmer is to cook a liquid or a food in a liquid with gentle heat just below the boiling point. Small bubbles slowly rising to the surface of the liquid indicate simmering.

Sliver: To sliver is the technique of cutting food into thin strips or pieces. Basil and garlic are two ingredients that may be identified as slivered in a recipe.

Strain: Straining refers to the technique of pouring a liquid through the small holes of a strainer or the wire mesh of a sieve to remove lumps or unwanted particles.

Toast: Toasting is the technique of browning foods by means of dry heat. Bread products, nuts, seeds, and coconut are commonly toasted. Toasting is done in a toaster, toaster oven, oven, or skillet, or under the broiler. The purpose of toasting bread is to brown, crisp, and dry it. Nuts, seeds, and coconut are toasted to intensify their flavor.

Whip: To whip refers to the technique of beating ingredients such as egg whites and whipping cream with a wire whisk or electric mixer in order to incorporate air and increase their volume. This results in a light, fluffy texture.

Whisk: Whisking is the technique of stirring, beating, or whipping foods with a wire whisk or electric hand or stand mixer. If you do not have a whisk, you can use a wooden spoon if the purpose is to blend ingredients.

BARS & BROWNIES

Simple and sweet, bars and brownies are the perfect afternoon treat

MOCHA FUDGE BROWNIES

MAKES 16 BROWNIES

- 3 **squares (1 ounce each) semisweet chocolate**
- ¾ **cup sugar**
- ½ **cup (1 stick) butter, softened**
- 2 **eggs**
- 2 **teaspoons instant espresso powder**
- 1 **teaspoon vanilla**
- ½ **cup all-purpose flour**
- ½ **cup chopped toasted almonds**
- 1 **cup (6 ounces) milk chocolate chips, divided**

1 Preheat oven to 350°F. Grease 8-inch square baking pan.

2 Melt semisweet chocolate in top of double boiler over hot, not boiling, water. Remove from heat; let cool slightly.

3 Beat sugar and butter in bowl of electric stand mixer until well blended. Add eggs; beat until light and fluffy. Add melted chocolate, espresso powder and vanilla; beat until well blended. Stir in flour, almonds and ½ cup chocolate chips. Spread batter evenly in prepared pan.

4 Bake 25 minutes or just until firm in center. Sprinkle with remaining ½ cup chocolate chips. Let stand until chips melt; spread chocolate evenly over brownies. Cool completely in pan on wire rack. Cut into 2-inch squares.

MEYER LEMON BARS

MAKES 12 BARS

CRUST

½ cup (1 stick) butter, softened
¼ cup sugar
1 cup all-purpose flour
Pinch salt

FILLING

3 eggs
1 cup sugar
Grated peel from 2 lemons
⅔ cup freshly squeezed Meyer lemon juice
¼ cup all-purpose flour
½ teaspoon salt
½ teaspoon baking soda

MERINGUE

1 tablespoon cornstarch
½ cup hot water
5 egg whites
½ teaspoon vanilla
¼ teaspoon cream of tartar
½ cup sugar

1 Preheat oven to 350°F. Spray 8-inch square pan with nonstick cooking spray. For crust, cream butter and sugar in bowl of electric stand mixer on low 1 to 2 minutes. Add flour and salt; beat until mixture begins to cling together.

2 Press dough evenly into bottom of prepared pan; bake 20 minutes or until edges become golden. Remove crust to cool; reduce oven temperature to 325°F.

3 Meanwhile, make filling. Place eggs in stand mixer. Beat 3 minutes or until pale and slightly thickened. Add sugar, lemon peel, lemon juice, flour, salt and baking soda. Mix on low 2 minutes or until smooth. Pour over crust; bake 20 minutes or until lightly set. Cool completely.

4 For meringue topping, place cornstarch in small saucepan; add enough water to make smooth paste. Add remaining water and heat until boiling. Cook, stirring constantly, about 1 minute or until thick paste forms; cool.

5 Raise oven temperature to 350°F. Attach wire whip and clean bowl to stand mixer. Whip egg whites, vanilla and cream of tartar at high speed until soft peaks form. Gradually beat in sugar; add cornstarch mixture by tablespoonfuls. Beat until stiff peaks form.

6 Spread meringue over lemon filling to cover completely. Bake about 10 minutes or until peaks are lightly browned.

TIP

Meyer lemons are slightly sweeter lemons found in the grocery store produce aisle.

GERMAN CHOCOLATE BROWNIES

MAKES 12 BROWNIES

4 ounces German baking chocolate

1 ounce unsweetened baking chocolate

⅔ cup butter

⅓ cup sugar

2 teaspoons vanilla

3 eggs

1 cup all-purpose flour

½ teaspoon salt

⅔ cup chopped pecans

Coconut-Pecan Frosting (recipe follows)

Candied Pecans (recipe follows)

TIP

German chocolate is dark, but sweeter than semisweet chocolate. It is named for its creator, a man named German, not the country.

1 Preheat oven to 350°F. Grease 9-inch square baking pan.

2 Melt chocolate and butter in small saucepan over low heat, stirring frequently. Cool slightly.

3 Place sugar, vanilla and eggs in bowl of electric stand mixer. Beat on high until combined. Turn mixer to low and slowly mix in chocolate mixture. Continuing on low, gradually mix in flour and salt until combined. Stir in pecans.

4 Spread batter in prepared pan. Bake 28 to 30 minutes or until toothpick inserted into center comes out clean. Cool completely. Frost with Coconut-Pecan Frosting and top with Candied Pecans.

COCONUT-PECAN FROSTING

2 egg yolks

6 ounces evaporated milk

¾ teaspoon vanilla

¾ cup packed light brown sugar

6 tablespoons butter

1⅓ cups flaked coconut

¾ cup chopped pecans

1 Whisk egg yolks, milk and vanilla in medium saucepan until well blended. Add sugar and butter; cook over low heat 10 to 12 minutes or until thickened, stirring frequently.

2 Remove from heat; mix in coconut and pecans. Cool completely.

CANDIED PECANS

- **2 tablespoons butter**
- **2 tablespoons packed brown sugar**
- **¾ cup whole pecans**

Melt butter and brown sugar in saucepan over medium heat. Stir in pecans. Cook and stir 1 minute or until pecans are coated with sugar mixture. Spread on waxed paper to cool.

SWEET POTATO COCONUT BARS

MAKES 24 BARS

CRUST

30 vanilla wafers, crushed

1½ cups finely chopped walnuts, toasted, divided

½ cup sweetened flaked coconut

¼ cup (½ stick) butter, softened

FILLING

2 cups cooked and mashed sweet potatoes, or 2 (16-ounce) cans, well-drained and mashed

2 eggs

1 teaspoon ground cinnamon

½ teaspoon ground ginger

¼ to ½ teaspoon ground cloves

¼ teaspoon salt

1 can (14 ounces) sweetened condensed milk

1 cup butterscotch chips

1 Preheat oven to 350°F.

2 For crust, combine vanilla wafers, 1 cup walnuts, coconut and butter in medium bowl until well blended. (Mixture will be dry and crumbly.) Place two thirds of mixture in bottom of 13×9-inch baking pan, pressing down lightly to form even layer.

3 For filling, beat mashed sweet potatoes, eggs, cinnamon, ginger, cloves and salt in bowl of electric stand mixer at medium-low speed until well blended. Gradually add milk; beat until well blended. Spoon filling evenly over crust. Top with remaining crust mixture, pressing lightly into sweet potato layer.

4 Bake 25 to 30 minutes or until knife inserted into center comes out clean. Sprinkle with butterscotch chips and remaining ½ cup walnuts. Bake 2 minutes more. Cool completely in pan on wire rack. Cover with plastic wrap and refrigerate 2 to 3 hours before serving.

CRUSHING VANILLA WAFERS

Vanilla wafers can be crushed in a food processor or in a resealable food storage bag with a rolling pin or mallet. Crush the wafers until the crumbs are a uniform size for the best consistency.

SPIKED CHEESECAKE BARS

MAKES 24 BARS

CRUST

½ **cup packed light brown sugar**

⅓ **cup butter, softened**

¾ **cup plus 1 teaspoon all-purpose flour, divided**

¾ **cup quick oats**

¼ **teaspoon baking soda**

FILLING

1 **package (8 ounces) cream cheese, softened**

¼ **cup granulated sugar**

¼ **cup any flavored liqueur, such as coffee, orange or hazelnut**

2 **tablespoons milk**

1 **egg**

¼ **cup semisweet chocolate chips**

TIP

When cutting cheesecake, wipe the knife blade clean between cuts for smoother, neater bars or slices.

1 Preheat oven to 350°F. Line bottom and sides of 8-inch square baking pan with foil, leaving 2-inch overhang.

2 For crust, beat brown sugar and butter in bowl of electric stand mixer at medium-high speed until creamy. Combine ¾ cup flour, oats and baking soda in small bowl; gradually beat into sugar mixture at low speed until blended. (Mixture will be crumbly.) Lightly press onto bottom of prepared pan to form crust. Bake 20 to 25 minutes or until golden brown. Set aside on wire rack.

3 Meanwhile, for filling, combine cream cheese, granulated sugar, liqueur and milk in clean mixer bowl; beat at medium-high speed until smooth. Add egg and remaining 1 teaspoon flour; beat until well blended. Spoon filling over hot crust. Bake 38 to 43 minutes or until set. Cool completely in pan on wire rack.

4 Place chocolate chips in small resealable food storage bag; microwave on HIGH 30 seconds or until slightly melted. Knead bag; microwave 20 seconds or until completely melted. Cut tiny hole in corner of bag and drizzle chocolate over cooled cheesecake. Cover with foil and refrigerate overnight for best flavor and texture. Remove cheesecake from pan using foil handles; place on cutting board and cut into bars.

ORANGE MARMALADE BARS

MAKES 24 BARS

SHORTBREAD CRUST

- ¼ **cup hazelnuts, toasted, skins removed***
- 1 **cup all-purpose flour**
- ¼ **cup packed brown sugar**
- 6 **tablespoons cold butter, cut into pieces**
- 1 **egg**
- 1 **teaspoon vanilla**

FILLING

- 1 **cup plus 2 teaspoons orange marmalade, divided**
- 4 **ounces cream cheese**
- ¼ **cup heavy cream**
- 1 **tablespoon granulated sugar**
- 1 **tablespoon grated orange peel**
- ½ **cup hazelnuts, toasted, skins removed***
- 2 **tablespoons packed brown sugar**
- 1 **teaspoon all-purpose flour**
- 2 **tablespoons melted butter**

Bake 5 minutes in a 300°F oven. Place nuts inside a towel and roll to release skins.

1 Preheat oven to 375°F. Grease 13×9-inch baking pan.

2 For crust, grind hazelnuts in food processor. Add flour and brown sugar; pulse to combine. Add butter; pulse until mixture resembles coarse crumbs. Add egg and vanilla; pulse just until dough forms.

3 Press dough evenly into prepared pan. Bake 12 to 15 minutes or until crust is golden brown.

4 Spread 1 cup marmalade evenly over hot crust.

5 Place cream cheese, cream, granulated sugar, remaining 2 teaspoons marmalade and orange peel in bowl of electric stand mixer. Mix at low speed until smooth and creamy. Finely chop hazelnuts. Toss nuts with brown sugar, flour and melted butter until nuts are evenly coated.

6 Pour cream cheese mixture over marmalade and crust. Sprinkle hazelnut topping evenly over filling. Bake 12 to 15 minutes or until topping is lightly browned and filling bubbles slightly.

7 Cool on wire rack for 2 hours. Use sharp knife to cut into 2-inch bars.

MORNING SANDWICHES

MAKES 6 SANDWICHES

1 tablespoon butter or
  vegetable oil

¾ cup quick oats

¼ cup sliced almonds

1 cup whole wheat flour

1 cup peeled and grated
  apple

1 cup shredded carrots

⅓ cup cholesterol-free egg
  substitute*

¼ cup pitted and chopped
  prunes

¼ cup fat-free (skim) milk

2 tablespoons sugar
  substitute

½ teaspoon baking powder

½ teaspoon ground cinnamon

¼ teaspoon baking soda

¼ teaspoon ground nutmeg

6 teaspoons reduced-fat
  peanut butter

6 teaspoons sugar-free
  raspberry preserves

*If you'd prefer, substitute 1 egg for the
⅓ cup cholesterol-free egg substitute.*

1 Preheat oven to 425°F. Spray 13×9-inch baking pan with nonstick cooking spray; set aside.

2 Melt butter in small nonstick saucepan over medium heat. Add oats and almonds; cook and stir 3 minutes. Remove from heat and let cool.

3 Place oat mixture, flour, apple, carrots, egg substitute, prunes, milk, sugar substitute, baking powder, cinnamon, baking soda and nutmeg in food processor; pulse until combined.

4 Press dough evenly into prepared pan. Bake 20 minutes. Cool 15 minutes in pan on wire rack.

5 Cut into 12 pieces. Spread 6 pieces with peanut butter. Spread remaining 6 pieces with raspberry preserves. Top raspberry pieces with peanut butter pieces to make sandwiches.

SLICED ALMONDS

Don't try to slice whole almonds yourself. Instead, look for pre-sliced or slivered almonds in the baking aisle of your local grocery store. If you have extra left over, add them to salads or muffins for a healthful, tasty crunch.

WHITE CHOCOLATE PEPPERMINT BROWNIES

MAKES 12 BROWNIES

BROWNIES

1 package (12 ounces) white chocolate chips, divided

¼ cup granulated sugar

3 eggs

½ cup (1 stick) butter, melted

1¼ cups all-purpose flour

½ teaspoon salt

½ cup crushed peppermint candies

FROSTING

6 tablespoons butter

3 tablespoons cream cheese

1¼ cups powdered sugar

Crushed peppermint candies

1 Preheat oven to 350°F. Grease 9-inch square baking pan. Melt 1 cup chips in small saucepan over low heat, stirring constantly until smooth. Cool slightly.

2 Beat granulated sugar and eggs in bowl of electric stand mixer at medium-high speed 5 minutes. Turn to low speed and blend in melted chocolate, butter, flour and salt. Stir in crushed candy.

3 Spread batter into prepared pan. Bake 20 to 25 minutes or until toothpick inserted into center comes out clean. Cool completely on wire rack.

4 Meanwhile, prepare frosting. Melt remaining chips in small saucepan over low heat, stirring constantly until smooth. Cool slightly. Beat butter, cream cheese and powdered sugar in mixer bowl until smooth. Beat in melted chocolate.

5 Frost brownies and sprinkle with crushed peppermint candies.

DARK CHOCOLATE NUT BARS

MAKES ABOUT 48 BARS

1 Preheat oven to 350°F. Grease 13×9-inch baking pan. Chop candy into ¼-inch chunks; place in refrigerator until ready to use.

2 Combine flour, cocoa, baking powder and salt in small bowl. Beat butter, brown sugar and granulated sugar in bowl of electric stand mixer until creamy. Beat in eggs and vanilla until well blended. Stir in flour mixture.

3 Reserve half of chopped candy; stir remaining candy and pecans into dough. Spread dough in prepared pan. Sprinkle with reserved candy.

4 Bake about 25 minutes or until toothpick inserted into center comes out clean. Cut into 1½-inch bars.

1   **package (12 ounces) dark chocolate almond nuggets***
1½ **cups all-purpose flour**
⅓   **cup unsweetened Dutch process cocoa powder**
1½ **teaspoons baking powder**
½   **teaspoon salt**
1   **cup (2 sticks) butter, softened**
¾   **cup packed brown sugar**
½   **cup granulated sugar**
2   **eggs**
1   **teaspoon vanilla**
1   **cup chopped pecans**

Or substitute your favorite candy bar, enough to make 1½ cups chopped candy.

CHOCOLATE RASPBERRY BARS

MAKES 16 BARS

1⅓ cups all-purpose flour

1 cup quick or old-fashioned oats

⅓ cup unsweetened cocoa powder

1 teaspoon baking powder

½ teaspoon salt

¼ teaspoon baking soda

1 cup packed brown sugar

½ cup (1 stick) butter, softened

2 eggs

1 cup mini candy-coated chocolate pieces

⅓ cup seedless raspberry jam

1 Preheat oven to 350°F. Grease 9-inch square baking pan.

2 Combine flour, oats, cocoa, baking powder, salt and baking soda in medium bowl. Beat brown sugar and butter in bowl of electric stand mixer at medium speed until smooth and creamy. Beat in eggs until well blended. Add flour mixture; beat until blended. Stir in chocolate candies.

3 Reserve 1 cup dough; spread remaining dough in prepared pan. Spread jam evenly over dough to within ½ inch of edges of pan. Drop teaspoonfuls of reserved dough over jam.

4 Bake 25 to 30 minutes or until bars are slightly firm near edges. Cool completely on wire rack.

CARAMEL CHOCOLATE CHUNK BLONDIES

MAKES ABOUT 2½ DOZEN BLONDIES

1 Preheat oven to 350°F. Spray 13×9-inch baking pan with nonstick cooking spray.

2 Combine flour, baking powder and salt in medium bowl. Beat granulated sugar, brown sugar and butter in bowl of electric stand mixer at medium speed until smooth and creamy. Beat in eggs and vanilla until well blended. Add flour mixture; beat at low speed until blended. Stir in chocolate chunks.

3 Spread batter evenly in prepared pan. Drop spoonfuls of caramel topping over batter; swirl into batter with knife.

4 Bake 25 minutes or until golden brown. Cool completely in pan on wire rack.

- 1½ **cups all-purpose flour**
- 1 **teaspoon baking powder**
- ½ **teaspoon salt**
- ¾ **cup granulated sugar**
- ¾ **cup packed brown sugar**
- ½ **cup (1 stick) butter, softened**
- 2 **eggs**
- 1½ **teaspoons vanilla**
- 1½ **cups semisweet chocolate chunks**
- ⅓ **cup caramel ice cream topping**

GINGERBREAD CHEESECAKE BARS

MAKES 24 BARS

- 1 **package (8 ounces) cream cheese, softened**
- ⅔ **cup sugar, divided**
- 3 **eggs, divided**
- 1½ **teaspoons ground ginger, divided**
- ½ **teaspoon vanilla**
- ½ **cup (1 stick) butter, softened**
- ¾ **cup molasses**
- 2 **cups all-purpose flour**
- 1 **teaspoon baking soda**
- ¾ **teaspoon ground cinnamon**
- ¼ **teaspoon salt**
- ¼ **teaspoon ground allspice**

1 Preheat oven to 350°F. Grease 13×9-inch baking pan.

2 Beat cream cheese and ⅓ cup sugar in bowl of electric stand mixer at medium speed until light and fluffy. Add 1 egg, ½ teaspoon ginger and vanilla; beat until well blended and smooth. Refrigerate until ready to use.

3 Beat butter and remaining ⅓ cup sugar in clean mixer bowl at medium speed until light and fluffy. Add molasses and remaining 2 eggs; beat until well blended. Combine flour, baking soda, remaining 1 teaspoon ginger, cinnamon, salt and allspice in small bowl. Add flour mixture to butter mixture; beat just until blended. Spread batter evenly in prepared pan. Drop cream cheese mixture by spoonfuls onto gingerbread batter; swirl into batter with knife.

4 Bake 25 to 30 minutes or until toothpick inserted into center comes out clean. Cool completely in pan on wire rack. Cut into bars.

CARROT & SPICE BARS

MAKES 40 BARS

1 Preheat oven to 350°F. Lightly coat 13×9-inch baking pan with nonstick cooking spray.

2 Combine milk and butter in large microwavable bowl. Microwave on HIGH 1 minute or until butter is melted; add cereal. Let stand 5 minutes. Pour milk mixture into bowl of electric stand mixer. Add eggs; mix on low to blend. Add puréed carrots, grated carrot, raisins, orange peel and vanilla.

3 Combine flour, sugar, baking soda and cinnamon in bowl. Add to carrot mixture, mixing on low until thoroughly blended. Spread into prepared pan.

4 Bake 25 minutes or until toothpick inserted into center comes out clean. Insert tines of fork into cake at 1-inch intervals. Spoon orange juice over cake. Sprinkle with pecans; press into cake. Cut into 40 bars before serving.

- 1 **cup low-fat (1%) milk**
- ¼ **cup (½ stick) butter**
- 1 **cup bran flakes cereal**
- 2 **eggs**
- 1 **jar (2½ ounces) puréed baby food carrots**
- ¾ **cup grated carrot**
- ⅓ **cup golden raisins, coarsely chopped**
- 1 **teaspoon grated orange peel**
- 1 **teaspoon vanilla**
- 2 **cups all-purpose flour**
- ¾ **cup sugar**
- 1 **teaspoon baking soda**
- 1 **teaspoon ground cinnamon**
- ¼ **cup orange juice**
- ¼ **cup toasted pecans, chopped**

SHORTBREAD TURTLE COOKIE BARS
MAKES ABOUT 4½ DOZEN BARS

1¼ **cups (2½ sticks) butter, softened, divided**

1 **cup all-purpose flour**

1 **cup old-fashioned oats**

1¼ **cups packed brown sugar, divided**

1 **teaspoon ground cinnamon**

¼ **teaspoon salt**

1½ **cups chopped pecans**

4 **squares (1 ounce each) white chocolate, finely chopped**

6 **squares (1 ounce each) bittersweet or semisweet chocolate, finely chopped**

1 Preheat oven to 350°F.

2 Beat ½ cup butter in bowl of electric stand mixer at medium speed 2 minutes or until light and fluffy. Add flour, oats, ¾ cup brown sugar, cinnamon and salt; beat at low speed until coarse crumbs form. Pat firmly onto bottom of ungreased 13×9-inch baking pan. Set aside.

3 Heat remaining ¾ cup butter and ¾ cup brown sugar in heavy medium saucepan over medium-high heat, stirring constantly until butter melts. Bring mixture to a boil; cook 1 minute without stirring. Remove from heat; stir in pecans. Pour over crust.

4 Bake 18 to 22 minutes on center rack of oven or until caramel begins to bubble. Immediately sprinkle with white and bittersweet chocolates; swirl (do not spread) with knife after 45 seconds to 1 minute or when slightly softened. Cool completely in pan on wire rack; cut into 2×1-inch bars.

PEANUT BUTTER CHIP BROWNIES

MAKES 16 BROWNIES

1 Preheat oven to 350°F. Grease 8-inch square baking pan.

2 Combine flour, cocoa, baking powder and salt in medium bowl. Combine brown sugar, granulated sugar and melted butter in bowl of electric stand mixer; mix on low until well blended. Add eggs; mix on medium-low until well blended. Stir in flour mixture, peanut butter chips and peanuts; mix well. Spread evenly in prepared pan.

3 Bake 30 to 35 minutes or until edges of brownies begin to pull away from sides of pan. Cool completely in pan on wire rack.

- 1 **cup all-purpose flour**
- ⅓ **cup unsweetened Dutch process cocoa powder**
- ½ **teaspoon baking powder**
- ½ **teaspoon salt**
- 1 **cup packed brown sugar**
- ½ **cup granulated sugar**
- ½ **cup (1 stick) butter, melted**
- 2 **eggs, lightly beaten**
- 1 **cup peanut butter chips**
- ½ **cup chopped peanuts**

KEY LIME BARS

MAKES 24 BARS

CRUST

1½ **cups finely crushed graham crackers (10 to 12 crackers)**

¼ **cup packed brown sugar**

2 **tablespoons all-purpose flour**

5 **tablespoons melted butter**

FILLING

8 **ounces cream cheese, softened**

1½ **cups granulated sugar**

2 **eggs**

¼ **cup freshly squeezed Key lime juice**

1 **tablespoon grated lime peel**

TIP

If Key limes aren't available, look for bottled Key lime juice in the juice aisle of large supermarkets and specialty food stores.

1 Preheat oven to 350°F. Grease 13×9-inch baking pan.

2 For crust, combine graham cracker crumbs, brown sugar and flour in large bowl. Add melted butter to cracker mixture in two parts, stirring until the mixture is thoroughly moist and crumbly.

3 Reserve ¼ cup crumbs to top bars, if desired. Press crust evenly into prepared pan and bake 15 minutes; set aside.

4 For filling, place cream cheese and granulated sugar in bowl of electric stand mixer. Beat at medium-low speed until smooth and creamy. Add eggs, one at a time, beating well after each addition. Add lime juice and lime peel. Mix until just combined.

5 Pour filling over warm crust. Bake in center of oven 15 to 20 minutes or until filling is set and begins to pull away from sides of pan.

6 Sprinkle reserved crust crumbs evenly over filling, if desired. Cool on wire rack 2 hours. Using sharp knife, cut into 2-inch bars.

CAKES & FROSTINGS

A triple-layered sweet masterpiece
will be in your baking repertoire

DOUBLE CHOCOLATE POUND CAKE

MAKES 10 SERVINGS

CAKE

- 3 **cups all-purpose flour**
- 2 **cups granulated sugar**
- ½ **cup unsweetened Dutch process cocoa powder**
- 3 **teaspoons baking powder**
- ½ **teaspoon salt**
- 1 **cup (2 sticks) butter, softened**
- 1¼ **cups milk**
- 1 **teaspoon vanilla**
- 5 **eggs**

CHOCOLATE GLAZE

- 2 **squares (1 ounce each) unsweetened chocolate**
- 3 **tablespoons butter**
- 1 **cup powdered sugar**
- ¾ **teaspoon vanilla**
- 2 **tablespoons hot water**

1 Preheat oven to 325°F. Grease and flour 12-cup bundt pan.

2 Combine dry ingredients in bowl of electric stand mixer. Add butter, milk and vanilla. Mix on low speed about 1 minute. Stop and scrape bowl. Turn to medium-high and beat about 2 minutes. Stop and scrape bowl. Turn to low and add eggs, one at a time, mixing about 15 seconds after each addition. Turn to medium and beat about 30 seconds.

3 Pour batter into prepared pan. Bake 1 hour and 5 minutes or until toothpick inserted near center comes out clean. Cool completely on wire rack. Remove cake from pan.

4 For Chocolate Glaze, melt chocolate and butter in small saucepan over low heat. Remove from heat. Stir in powdered sugar and vanilla. Stir in water, 1 teaspoon at a time, until glaze is desired consistency. Drizzle over cake.

SUNSHINE CHIFFON CAKE

MAKES 10 SERVINGS

2 cups all-purpose flour

1½ cups sugar

1 tablespoon baking powder

½ teaspoon salt

¾ cup cold water

½ cup vegetable oil

7 eggs, separated

1 teaspoon vanilla

2 teaspoons grated lemon peel

½ teaspoon cream of tartar

Lemon Glaze (recipe follows)

1 Preheat oven to 325°F.

2 Attach wire whip to stand mixer. Combine flour, sugar, baking powder and salt in mixer bowl. Add water, vegetable oil, egg yolks, vanilla and lemon peel. Beat at medium speed about 1 minute. Stop and scrape bowl. Continuing on medium, beat about 15 seconds. Pour mixture into another bowl. Clean mixer bowl and wire whip.

3 Place egg whites and cream of tartar in mixer bowl. Turn to high and whip 2 to 2½ minutes or until whites are stiff but not dry. Remove bowl from mixer. Gradually fold batter into egg whites with spatula just until blended. Pour into ungreased 10-inch tube pan.

4 Bake 60 to 75 minutes or until top springs back when lightly touched. Immediately invert cake onto funnel or bottle if pan does not have built-in feet. Cool completely. Remove from pan. Drizzle with Lemon Glaze.

Lemon Glaze: Combine 1 cup powdered sugar and 1 tablespoon softened butter in small bowl. Stir in 2 to 3 tablespoons lemon juice, 1 tablespoon at a time, until glaze is desired consistency.

WHOOPIE PIES

MAKES 8 PIES

2 cups flour
1½ teaspoons baking soda
1 teaspoon salt
½ cup (1 stick) butter
¾ cup packed light brown
  sugar
¼ cup granulated sugar
1 egg
1 teaspoon vanilla
1 cup buttermilk
  **Marshmallow-Buttercream
  Filling (recipe follows)**

TIP

Drop the batter onto the parchment with a measuring cup instead of a spoon or ladle. Simply dip the cup into the bowl, level off the batter and pour slowly.

1 Preheat oven to 350°F. Combine flour, baking soda and salt in small bowl; set aside.

2 Cream butter and sugars in bowl of electric stand mixer at medium-high. Add egg and vanilla; beat until well combined.

3 Alternately add flour mixture and buttermilk, stirring after each addition.

4 Line cookie sheet with parchment paper; grease well. Drop scant ¼ cups of batter onto parchment paper 3 inches apart. Bake 10 to 12 minutes or until cakes are set. Cool completely.

5 Prepare Marshmallow-Buttercream Filling. Spread 3 tablespoons filling onto flat side of half the cakes. Top with remaining cakes.

MARSHMALLOW-BUTTERCREAM FILLING

½ cup (1 stick) butter
¾ cup powdered sugar
7 ounces marshmallow creme
1 teaspoon vanilla

1 Cream butter and powdered sugar in mixer bowl until light and fluffy.

2 Add marshmallow creme and vanilla; beat until smooth.

RASPBERRY-CREAM JELLY-ROLL CAKE

MAKES 12 SERVINGS

SPONGE SHEET CAKE

- **3 tablespoons butter, divided**
  Powdered sugar
- **1 cup all-purpose flour**
- **1 teaspoon baking powder**
- **½ teaspoon salt**
- **⅓ cup milk**
- **½ teaspoon vanilla**
- **6 eggs**
- **1 cup granulated sugar**

FILLING

- **1 cup cold whipping cream**
- **½ teaspoon vanilla**
- **3 tablespoons sugar**
  Brandy or rum
- **¾ cup raspberry jam**

TIP

For best results, use a large flat-weave kitchen towel to roll the cake.

1 For Sponge Sheet Cake, preheat oven to 350°F. Spray 17×11-inch jelly-roll pan with nonstick cooking spray. Line with parchment paper; grease paper with 1 tablespoon butter and dust with powdered sugar.

2 Sift flour, baking powder and salt into bowl. Heat milk, remaining 2 tablespoons butter and vanilla in small saucepan over low heat. Combine eggs and granulated sugar in mixer bowl. Whip at high speed until mixture triples in volume, about 5 minutes.

3 Gently mix milk mixture into egg mixture. Gradually add flour mixture, stirring at low speed after each addition until batter is smooth. Pour batter into prepared pan. Bake 15 minutes or until cake is lightly browned and center springs back when touched. Cool 5 minutes.

4 Generously dust large kitchen towel with powdered sugar. Run a knife around cake edges to loosen and invert onto towel. Cool 5 minutes.

5 Peel off parchment paper. Starting from short side, roll cake with towel inside as tightly as possible without cracking. Refrigerate 1 hour.

6 For filling, place cream and vanilla in cold mixer bowl. Whip at high speed until cream begins to thicken. Gradually sprinkle in sugar, whipping until stiff.

7 Unroll cake and brush inside generously with brandy. Stir jam until smooth; spread evenly over cake. Spread whipped cream over jam.

8 Roll cake tightly. Wrap and refrigerate several hours until firm. Sprinkle with powdered sugar just before serving, if desired.

CARROT CAKE

MAKES 10 SERVINGS

4 eggs
1 cup (2 sticks) butter, melted
2 cups all-purpose flour
1½ cups sugar
1½ teaspoons baking powder
1 teaspoon cinnamon
¼ teaspoon salt
2½ cups finely grated carrots
1½ cups chopped walnuts, divided
Cream Cheese Frosting (recipe follows)

CHOPPING WALNUTS

To quickly chop walnuts or any other type of nut, use a food processor fitted with a steel blade and pulse until evenly chopped.

1 Preheat oven to 350°F. Grease and flour 9-inch springform pan.

2 Place eggs and butter in bowl of electric stand mixer. Turn to medium-high and beat 1 minute. Stop and scrape bowl. Add flour, sugar, baking powder, cinnamon and salt. Turn to low and beat 30 seconds, until combined. Continuing on low, fold in carrots and ½ cup walnuts, about 10 seconds.

3 Pour batter into prepared pan. Bake 1 hour and 15 minutes. (Cake is very moist and should not be tested for doneness with an inserted toothpick.) Cool in pan 10 minutes. Remove from pan and cool completely on wire rack. Slice cake in half to form two layers.

4 Prepare Cream Cheese Frosting. Fill and frost cake. Press remaining 1 cup walnuts onto side of cake.

CREAM CHEESE FROSTING

4 packages (3 ounces each) cream cheese, softened
½ cup (1 stick) butter
2 teaspoons vanilla
2½ cups powdered sugar

1 Place cream cheese, butter and vanilla in mixer bowl. Turn to medium-high and beat 2 minutes. Stop and scrape bowl.

2 Sift powdered sugar into bowl. Turn to low and beat 30 seconds, just until combined. Stop and scrape bowl. Turn to medium-high and beat 2 minutes. Refrigerate until ready to use.

VELVETY COCONUT AND SPICE CAKE

MAKES 10 SERVINGS

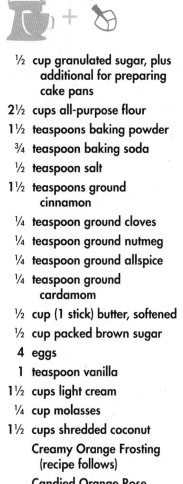

½ **cup granulated sugar, plus additional for preparing cake pans**

2½ **cups all-purpose flour**

1½ **teaspoons baking powder**

¾ **teaspoon baking soda**

½ **teaspoon salt**

1½ **teaspoons ground cinnamon**

¼ **teaspoon ground cloves**

¼ **teaspoon ground nutmeg**

¼ **teaspoon ground allspice**

¼ **teaspoon ground cardamom**

½ **cup (1 stick) butter, softened**

½ **cup packed brown sugar**

4 **eggs**

1 **teaspoon vanilla**

1½ **cups light cream**

¼ **cup molasses**

1½ **cups shredded coconut**

Creamy Orange Frosting (recipe follows)

Candied Orange Rose (recipe follows, optional)

⅔ **cup orange marmalade**

1 Preheat oven to 350°F. Grease 3 (8-inch) round cake pans; sprinkle with enough granulated sugar to lightly coat bottoms and sides of pans.

2 Combine flour, baking powder, baking soda, salt and spices in medium bowl; set aside.

3 Beat butter in bowl of electric stand mixer until creamy. Add ½ cup granulated sugar and brown sugar; beat until light and fluffy. Add eggs, one at a time, beating well after each addition. Blend in vanilla.

4 Combine cream and molasses in small bowl. Add flour mixture to egg mixture alternately with molasses mixture, beating well after each addition. Stir in coconut; pour evenly into prepared pans.

5 Bake 20 minutes or until toothpick inserted into centers comes out clean. Cool in pans on wire racks 10 minutes. Loosen edges; remove to racks to cool completely.

6 Prepare Creamy Orange Frosting and Candied Orange Rose, if desired.

7 To assemble, spread 2 cake layers with marmalade; stack on serving plate. Top with third cake layer. Frost with Creamy Orange Frosting. Refrigerate. Garnish, if desired.

CREAMY ORANGE FROSTING

- 1 (3-ounce) package cream cheese, softened
- 2 cups powdered sugar
  Few drops orange extract
  Milk (optional)

1 Beat cream cheese in bowl of electric stand mixer until creamy. Gradually add powdered sugar, beating until fluffy. Blend in orange extract.

2 If necessary, add milk, 1 teaspoonful at a time, for a thinner consistency.

CANDIED ORANGE ROSE

- 1 cup granulated sugar
- 1 cup water
- 1 orange

1 Combine sugar and water in medium saucepan. Bring to a boil over medium-high heat, stirring occasionally.

2 Meanwhile, thinly peel orange leaving as much membrane on orange as possible. Carefully roll up peel; secure with toothpick. Place on slotted spoon; add to hot sugar syrup.

3 Reduce heat to low; simmer 5 to 10 minutes or until orange peel turns translucent. Remove from syrup; place on waxed paper-lined cookie sheet to cool. Remove toothpick.

SAGE CAKE WITH HERBED STRAWBERRIES

MAKES 10 SERVINGS

**Herbed Strawberries
(recipe follows)**
- ⅔ cup milk
- 14 whole fresh sage leaves, divided
- 4 egg yolks
- 1 teaspoon vanilla
- 2 cups cake flour, sifted
- 1 cup sugar
- 1 tablespoon baking powder
- ½ teaspoon salt
- ½ cup (1 stick) butter, softened and cut into pieces

PAN PREPARATION

To grease and flour a pan, use a paper towel to coat the inside of the pan with butter or shortening. Then add a bit of flour to the pan and shake to coat evenly. Invert the pan and tap to remove excess flour.

1 Prepare Herbed Strawberries. Preheat oven to 350°F. Grease and flour 9-inch springform pan.

2 Place milk in microwavable bowl. Crush or twist 6 sage leaves, tear them in half, and add to milk. Microwave mixture on HIGH 2 minutes or until very hot. Set aside to steep 15 minutes, then refrigerate until milk is cold. Strain milk through fine-mesh strainer.

3 Combine ⅓ cup of strained milk, egg yolks and vanilla in small bowl. Combine flour, sugar, baking powder and salt in bowl of electric stand mixer. With mixer on low, add butter in small pieces. Add remaining ⅓ cup milk until ingredients are moistened. Gradually beat in egg mixture on low speed. Increase speed to medium and beat 1 minute until light and fluffy.

4 Pour batter into prepared pan and arrange remaining sage leaves on top of batter. Bake 28 to 30 minutes or until cake is lightly golden and starts to pull away from edge of pan. Cool on rack 10 minutes. Remove side of pan and transfer to serving platter. Spoon Herbed Strawberries and juices onto cake slices, if desired.

Serving Suggestion: The flavors of the herbs in this dessert go particularly well with a cup of Earl Grey tea.

HERBED STRAWBERRIES

- 1 **pound fresh strawberries, washed, hulled and quartered**
- 1 **tablespoon chopped fresh thyme leaves**
- 1 **tablespoon sugar**
- 1 **teaspoon red wine vinegar**
- ⅛ **teaspoon freshly ground black pepper**

Combine all ingredients in medium bowl; let stand at room temperature at least 30 minutes or refrigerate up to 24 hours.

OLD-FASHIONED DEVIL'S FOOD CAKE

MAKES 10 SERVINGS

- **6 tablespoons butter, softened**
- **1½ cups sugar**
- **3 eggs**
- **1½ teaspoons vanilla**
- **2 cups cake flour**
- **½ cup unsweetened cocoa powder**
- **2 teaspoons baking powder**
- **½ teaspoon salt**
- **½ teaspoon baking soda**
- **1 cup buttermilk**
- **Creamy Chocolate Frosting (recipe follows)**

1 Preheat oven to 350°F. Grease and flour 3 (8-inch) round cake pans.

2 Beat butter and sugar in bowl of electric stand mixer at medium speed until fluffy. Beat in eggs and vanilla.

3 Combine flour, cocoa, baking powder, salt and baking soda in medium bowl. Add to butter mixture alternately with buttermilk, beating well after each addition.

4 Spread batter evenly in prepared pans. Bake 25 to 30 minutes or until toothpick inserted into centers comes out clean. Cool in pans on wire racks 10 minutes; remove from pans and cool completely.

5 Meanwhile, prepare Creamy Chocolate Frosting.

6 Place one cake layer on serving plate; spread with frosting. Repeat with remaining cake layers and frosting. Frost side and top of cake.

CREAMY CHOCOLATE FROSTING

- **5 cups powdered sugar**
- **⅓ cup unsweetened cocoa powder**
- **4 to 6 tablespoons milk, divided**
- **2 tablespoons butter, softened**
- **1 teaspoon vanilla**

1 Combine powdered sugar, cocoa, 4 tablespoons milk, butter and vanilla in large bowl of electric stand mixer.

2 Mix at low speed until smooth, scraping bowl frequently. Stir in additional milk, 1 tablespoon at a time, until desired consistency is reached.

PUMPKIN CHEESECAKE WITH GINGERSNAP-PECAN CRUST

MAKES 10 TO 12 SERVINGS

CRUST

1¼ **cups gingersnap cookie crumbs (about 24 cookies)**

⅓ **cup pecans, very finely chopped**

¼ **cup granulated sugar**

¼ **cup (½ stick) butter, melted**

FILLING

3 **packages (8 ounces each) cream cheese, softened**

1 **cup packed light brown sugar**

1 **teaspoon ground cinnamon**

½ **teaspoon ground ginger**

¼ **teaspoon ground nutmeg**

2 **eggs**

2 **egg yolks**

1 **cup solid-pack pumpkin**

1 Preheat oven to 350°F. For crust, combine cookie crumbs, pecans, granulated sugar and butter in medium bowl; mix well. Press crumb mixture evenly on bottom of ungreased 9-inch springform pan. Bake 8 to 10 minutes or until golden brown.

2 Meanwhile for filling, beat cream cheese in bowl of electric stand mixer at medium speed until light and fluffy. Add brown sugar, cinnamon, ginger and nutmeg; beat until well blended. Beat in eggs and egg yolks, one at a time, beating well after each addition. Beat in pumpkin. Pour mixture into crust.

3 Bake 1 hour or until edges are set but center is still moist. Turn off oven; let cheesecake stand in oven with door ajar 30 minutes. Transfer to wire rack. Loosen edge of cheesecake from side of pan with thin metal spatula; cool completely in pan on wire rack.

4 Cover; refrigerate at least 24 hours or up to 48 hours before serving.

TIP

To help prevent the cheesecake from cracking while baking, place a pan of water in the oven to create moist heat.

FLUFFY FROSTING

MAKES 2 CUPS

1½ **cups sugar**
½ **cup water**
1½ **tablespoons light corn syrup**
½ **teaspoon cream of tartar**
½ **teaspoon salt**
2 **egg whites**
1½ **teaspoons vanilla**

FROSTING TECHNIQUE

Place the cake on a serving plate. Place strips of waxed paper under cake to keep plate clean. Using an offset spatula, spread frosting first on side of the cake and then on top, using the spatula to make swirls.

---

1 Place sugar, water, corn syrup, cream of tartar and salt in medium saucepan. Cook and stir over medium heat until sugar is completely dissolved, forming a syrup.

2 Place egg whites and vanilla in bowl of electric stand mixer. Turn to high and whip about 45 seconds, or until egg whites begin to hold shape. Continuing on high, slowly pour hot syrup into egg whites in a fine stream and whip about 5 minutes longer or until frosting loses its gloss and stands in stiff peaks. Frost cake immediately.

Fluffy Chocolate Frosting: Melt 3 squares (1 ounce each) unsweetened chocolate with sugar mixture. Proceed as directed above.

Fluffy Peppermint Frosting: Omit vanilla and add 1 teaspoon peppermint extract. Proceed as directed above. Stir in ¼ cup crushed peppermint candy.

Fluffy Amaretto Frosting: Omit vanilla and add 2½ teaspoons Amaretto liqueur. Proceed as directed above.

Fluffy Lemon Frosting: Omit vanilla and add 1 teaspoon lemon extract and 2 teaspoons grated lemon peel. Proceed as directed above.

BANANA CAKE

MAKES 12 TO 16 SERVINGS

2½ cups all-purpose flour

1 tablespoon baking soda

½ teaspoon salt

1 cup granulated sugar

¾ cup packed light brown sugar

½ cup (1 stick) butter, softened

2 eggs

1 teaspoon vanilla

3 ripe bananas, mashed (about 1⅔ cups)

⅔ cup buttermilk

Fluffy Chocolate Frosting (page 60)

1 Preheat oven to 350°F. Grease 2 (8-inch) round cake pans. Combine flour, baking soda and salt in medium bowl.

2 Beat granulated sugar, brown sugar and butter in bowl of electric stand mixer at medium speed until well blended. Add eggs and vanilla; beat well. Stir in bananas. Alternately add flour mixture and buttermilk; beat until well blended after each addition. Pour batter into prepared pans.

3 Bake 35 minutes or until toothpick inserted into centers comes out clean. Cool in pans 10 minutes. Remove to wire racks; cool completely.

4 Prepare Fluffy Chocolate Frosting; fill and frost cake.

BLACK BOTTOM CUPCAKES

MAKES 20 CUPCAKES

1 Preheat oven to 350°F. Line 20 standard (2½-inch) muffin cups with paper or foil baking cups. Beat cream cheese, 1 egg and ⅓ cup granulated sugar in small bowl until smooth and creamy; set aside.

2 Combine flour, brown sugar, cocoa, remaining ½ cup granulated sugar, baking powder, baking soda and salt in bowl of electric stand mixer; mix well. Whisk buttermilk, remaining 3 eggs, oil and vanilla in medium bowl until well blended; add to flour mixture. Beat about 2 minutes or until well blended.

3 Spoon batter into prepared muffin cups, filling about three-fourths full. Spoon heaping tablespoonfuls of cream cheese mixture over batter in each cup; gently swirl with tip of knife to marbleize.

4 Bake 20 to 25 minutes or until toothpick inserted into centers comes out clean. Cool cupcakes in pans 5 minutes. Remove from pans; cool completely on wire racks.

- **1 package (8 ounces) cream cheese, softened**
- **4 eggs, divided**
- **⅓ cup plus ½ cup granulated sugar, divided**
- **2 cups all-purpose flour**
- **1 cup packed brown sugar**
- **¾ cup unsweetened cocoa powder**
- **1 teaspoon baking powder**
- **½ teaspoon baking soda**
- **½ teaspoon salt**
- **1 cup buttermilk**
- **½ cup vegetable oil**
- **1½ teaspoons vanilla**

LEMON POPPY SEED BUNDT CAKE

MAKES 16 SERVINGS

1   **cup granulated sugar**

½   **cup (1 stick) butter, softened**

1   **egg, at room temperature**

2   **egg whites, at room temperature**

¾   **cup low-fat (1%) milk**

2   **teaspoons vanilla**

2   **cups all-purpose flour**

2   **tablespoons poppy seeds**

1   **tablespoon grated lemon peel**

2   **teaspoons baking powder**

¼   **teaspoon salt**

4½   **teaspoons powdered sugar**

1 Preheat oven to 350°F. Grease and flour 12-cup bundt pan.

2 Beat granulated sugar, butter, egg and egg whites in bowl of electric stand mixer at medium speed until well blended. Add milk and vanilla; mix well. Add flour, poppy seeds, lemon peel, baking powder and salt; beat about 2 minutes or until smooth. Pour batter into prepared pan.

3 Bake 30 minutes or until toothpick inserted near center comes out clean. Gently loosen cake from pan with knife; turn out onto wire rack. Cool completely. Sprinkle with powdered sugar. Cut into 16 pieces.

MARBLE CHEESECAKE

MAKES 10 SERVINGS

1 Preheat oven to 325°F. Stir together graham cracker crumbs, brown sugar and butter. Press mixture onto bottom of 9-inch springform pan.

2 Beat cream cheese, granulated sugar and vanilla in bowl of electric stand mixer at medium-high 2 minutes or until fluffy. Stop and scrape bowl. Turn to low speed and add eggs, one at a time, beating 15 seconds after each addition. Stop and scrape bowl. Turn to medium speed and beat 30 seconds.

3 Pour one third of cream cheese mixture into a small bowl. Add chocolate and mix well. Drop chocolate and plain batter by spoonfuls into prepared crust. Swirl lightly with a knife. Bake 1 hour and 30 minutes. Cool on wire rack 30 minutes; refrigerate at least 2 hours.

- **1 cup graham cracker crumbs**
- **¼ cup packed brown sugar**
- **3 tablespoons butter, melted**
- **4 packages (8 ounces each) cream cheese, softened**
- **1¾ cups granulated sugar**
- **2 teaspoons vanilla**
- **4 eggs**
- **2 squares (1 ounce each) unsweetened chocolate, melted**

MOLTEN CINNAMON-CHOCOLATE CAKES

MAKES 6 CAKES

6 **ounces semisweet chocolate**
¾ **cup (1½ sticks) butter**
1½ **cups powdered sugar**
4 **eggs**
6 **tablespoons all-purpose flour**
1½ **teaspoons vanilla**
¾ **teaspoon ground cinnamon**
  Powdered sugar

1 Preheat oven to 425°F. Spray 6 jumbo muffin cups or 6 (1-cup) custard cups with nonstick cooking spray.

2 Combine chocolate and butter in medium microwavable bowl; heat on HIGH 1½ minutes, stirring every 30 seconds, until melted and smooth. Place chocolate mixture in bowl of electric stand mixer. Mix in powdered sugar, eggs, flour, vanilla and cinnamon until well blended. Pour batter into prepared muffin cups, filling slightly more than half full.

3 Bake 13 minutes or until tops spring back when lightly touched. Let stand 1 minute; loosen sides with knife. Gently lift out cakes and invert onto serving plates; sprinkle with powdered sugar. Serve immediately.

COOKIES & CREAM CUPCAKES

MAKES 24 CUPCAKES

1 Preheat oven to 350°F. Lightly grease 24 standard (2½-inch) muffin cups or line with paper baking cups.

2 Sift flour, baking powder and salt together in bowl of electric stand mixer. Stir in sugar. Add milk, butter and vanilla; beat at low speed 30 seconds. Stop and scrape bowl. Beat at medium speed 2 minutes. Add egg whites; beat 2 minutes. Stir in 1 cup crushed cookies. Spoon batter into prepared muffin cups, filling two-thirds full.

3 Bake 20 to 25 minutes or until toothpick inserted into centers comes out clean. Cool in pans on wire racks 10 minutes. Remove cupcakes to racks; cool completely.

4 Frost cupcakes; garnish with additional crushed cookies.

2¼ cups all-purpose flour
1 tablespoon baking powder
½ teaspoon salt
1⅔ cups sugar
1 cup milk
½ cup (1 stick) butter, softened
2 teaspoons vanilla
3 egg whites
1 cup crushed chocolate sandwich cookies (about 10 cookies), plus additional for garnish
Fluffy Frosting (page 60)

COOKIES

Do your cookie jar a favor — fill it with childhood favorites and stunning new flavors

NEW ENGLAND RAISIN SPICE COOKIES

MAKE ABOUT 60 COOKIES

1 cup packed brown sugar
½ cup shortening
¼ cup (½ stick) butter
1 egg
⅓ cup molasses
2¼ cups all-purpose flour
2 teaspoons baking soda
1 teaspoon salt
¾ teaspoon ground cinnamon
¼ teaspoon ground ginger
¼ teaspoon ground cloves
⅛ teaspoon ground allspice
1½ cups raisins
Granulated sugar

1 Beat brown sugar, shortening and butter in bowl of electric stand mixer on medium speed until creamy. Add egg and molasses; beat until fluffy.

2 Combine all remaining ingredients except granulated sugar in separate bowl. Gradually stir into shortening mixture until just blended. Cover; refrigerate at least 2 hours.

3 Preheat oven to 350°F.

4 Scoop heaping tablespoonfuls of dough; roll into smooth balls. Roll in granulated sugar. Place on ungreased cookie sheets 1½ to 2 inches apart. Bake 8 to 10 minutes or until golden brown. Cool 1 minute on cookie sheets. Remove to wire racks; cool completely. Store in airtight container.

BLACK & WHITE SANDWICH COOKIES

MAKES 22 TO 24 COOKIES

COOKIES

1¼ cups (2½ sticks) unsalted
    butter

¾ cup superfine sugar

1½ teaspoons vanilla

2⅓ cups all-purpose flour,
    divided

 1 egg

¾ teaspoon salt

⅓ cup unsweetened cocoa
    powder

FILLING

½ cup (1 stick) butter

4 ounces cream cheese

2 cups plus 2 tablespoons
    powdered sugar

2 tablespoons unsweetened
    cocoa powder

COCOA POWDER

*Cocoa powder gives doughs
and frostings a rich chocolate
flavor and dark color.*

1 For cookies, beat butter and sugar until creamy (not fluffy) in bowl of electric stand mixer. Beat in egg and vanilla. Beat in 2 cups flour and salt at low speed until combined.

2 Remove half of dough to medium bowl; stir in remaining ⅓ cup flour. Add ⅓ cup cocoa powder to dough in mixer bowl; stir to combine.

3 Wrap doughs separately in plastic and refrigerate 30 minutes or until firm.

4 Preheat oven to 350°F. Roll plain dough on floured surface to ¼-inch thickness. Cut out 2-inch circles; place 2 inches apart on nonstick cookie sheet. Repeat with chocolate dough. Bake 8 to 10 minutes or until firm but not browned. Remove to wire rack; cool completely.

5 Meanwhile, prepare filling. Beat butter and cream cheese in mixer bowl until well blended. Beat in 2 cups powdered sugar until creamy. Remove half of filling to small bowl; stir in remaining 2 tablespoons powdered sugar. Add cocoa powder to mixer bowl; beat until smooth. Spread cooled white cookies with chocolate frosting and chocolate cookies with plain frosting. Press cookies together to form sandwiches.

BRANDY SNAPS WITH LEMON RICOTTA CREAM

MAKES 24 COOKIES

COOKIES

- ½ **cup sugar**
- ½ **cup (1 stick) butter**
- ⅓ **cup light corn syrup**
- 1 **cup all-purpose flour**
- 1 **tablespoon brandy or cognac**

FILLING

- ½ **cup (1 stick) butter, softened**
- ½ **cup ricotta cheese**
- ¼ **cup sugar**
- 2 **teaspoons grated lemon peel**
- 1 **tablespoon lemon juice**

1 Preheat oven to 325°F. For cookies, place ½ cup sugar, ½ cup butter and corn syrup in medium saucepan over medium heat; cook and stir until butter is melted and mixture is blended. Stir in flour and brandy.

2 Drop level tablespoonfuls of batter about 3 inches apart onto ungreased cookie sheets, spacing to fit 4 cookies per sheet. Bake 1 cookie sheet at a time about 12 minutes or until golden brown.

3 Cool cookies 1 minute. To form into tubes, remove each cookie from baking sheet and loosely wrap around wooden spoon handle until cookie is almost cool.

4 For filling, place ½ cup butter, ricotta, ¼ cup sugar, lemon peel and lemon juice in food processor; process until smooth.

5 Place filling in pastry bag fitted with plain or star tip, or in 1-quart food storage bag with small corner cut off. Fill cookies just before serving.

USING A PASTRY BAG

Experiment with different shaped pastry bag tips, and see how easy it is to pipe beautiful fillings and decorations for your desserts.

CHOCOLATE COCONUT ALMOND MACAROONS

MAKES 18 COOKIES

1⅓ **cups flaked sweetened coconut (3½-ounce package)**

⅔ **cup sugar**

2 **egg whites**

½ **teaspoon vanilla**

¼ **teaspoon almond extract**
 Pinch salt

4 **ounces sliced almonds, coarsely crushed**

18 **whole almonds**
 Chocolate Ganache (recipe follows)

CHOCOLATE GANACHE

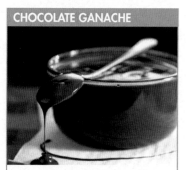

Chocolate ganache is a rich and decadent way to add a special touch to cookies and cakes. Try dipping other cookies in ganache, or drizzle over pound cake for a sinful treat.

1 Combine coconut, sugar, egg whites, vanilla, almond extract and salt in bowl of electric stand mixer; mix well. Fold in sliced almonds. Cover and refrigerate at least 1 hour or overnight.

2 Preheat oven to 350°F. Line baking sheet with parchment paper. Roll dough by tablespoonfuls into balls. Place 1 inch apart on prepared sheet. Press whole almond on top of each cookie. Bake 15 minutes or until light brown. Cool cookies 5 minutes on baking sheet. Transfer to wire rack; cool completely.

3 Meanwhile, prepare Chocolate Ganache; let cool 10 to 15 minutes.

4 Dip bottom of each cookie into ganache. Place cookies onto clean parchment or waxed paper-lined baking sheet. Refrigerate until ganache is firm. Store, covered, in refrigerator.

Chocolate Ganache: Place ½ cup semisweet chocolate chips in shallow bowl. Heat ¼ cup whipping cream in small saucepan until bubbles form around edges. Pour cream over chocolate; let stand 5 minutes. Stir until smooth.

OATMEAL S'MORES COOKIES

MAKES 40 COOKIES

⅔ **cup mini marshmallows**

2 **cups old-fashioned oats**

1⅓ **cups all-purpose flour**

¾ **teaspoon baking soda**

½ **teaspoon baking powder**

½ **teaspoon salt**

1 **cup packed brown sugar**

¾ **cup (1½ sticks) butter, softened**

¼ **cup granulated sugar**

1 **egg**

1 **tablespoon honey**

1 **teaspoon vanilla**

1 **cup semisweet chocolate chips**

¾ **cup coarse chocolate graham cracker crumbs**

1 Cut marshmallows in half. Spread on baking sheet; freeze 1 hour.

2 Preheat oven to 350°F. Line cookie sheets with parchment paper.

3 Combine oats, flour, baking soda, baking powder and salt in medium bowl. Beat brown sugar, butter and granulated sugar in bowl of electric stand mixer at medium speed until well blended. Beat at high speed until light and fluffy. Add egg, honey and vanilla; beat at medium speed until well blended. Gradually add flour mixture; beat just until blended. Stir in chocolate chips and frozen marshmallows.

4 Drop dough by rounded tablespoonfuls onto prepared cookie sheets; sprinkle with graham cracker crumbs. Bake 14 to 16 minutes or until puffed and golden. Cool 5 minutes on cookie sheets. Remove to wire racks to cool completely.

Variation: To make sandwich cookies, spread 1 tablespoon marshmallow creme onto flat side of 1 cookie. Spread 1 tablespoon prepared chocolate fudge frosting on flat side of second cookie. Press cookies together lightly; repeat with remaining cookies, marshmallow creme and frosting. Makes about 20 sandwiches.

DEEP DARK CHOCOLATE CHIP COOKIES

MAKES ABOUT 30 COOKIES

2 **packages (12 ounces each) semisweet chocolate chips, divided**

½ **cup (1 stick) butter, cut into chunks**

2 **eggs**

1 **teaspoon vanilla**

¾ **cup plus 2 tablespoons sugar**

⅔ **cup all-purpose flour**

2 **tablespoons unsweetened Dutch process cocoa powder**

1 **teaspoon baking powder**

¼ **teaspoon salt**

1 Lightly grease cookie sheets or line with parchment paper.

2 Combine 1 package (2 cups) chocolate chips and butter in large microwavable bowl. Microwave on HIGH 30 seconds; stir. Repeat as necessary until chips are melted and mixture is smooth. Let cool slightly.

3 Beat eggs and vanilla in bowl of electric stand mixer at medium speed until blended and frothy. Add sugar; beat until thick and light. Add chocolate mixture; beat until blended. Add flour, cocoa, baking powder and salt; beat until blended. Stir in remaining chocolate chips. (Dough will be soft.)

4 Drop dough by rounded tablespoonfuls 1½ inches apart onto prepared cookie sheets. Refrigerate 30 minutes.

5 Preheat oven to 325°F. Bake 16 to 20 minutes or until cookies are firm to the touch. Cool on cookie sheets 2 minutes. Remove to wire racks; cool completely.

COCONUT ALMOND BISCOTTI

MAKES 24 BISCOTTI

2½ cups all-purpose flour

1⅓ cups unsweetened shredded coconut

¾ cup sliced almonds

⅔ cup sugar

2 teaspoons baking powder

½ teaspoon salt

1 extra-large egg at room temperature

1 extra-large egg white at room temperature

8 tablespoons (1 stick) butter, melted

1 teaspoon vanilla

1 Center rack in oven and preheat to 350°F. Line baking sheet with parchment paper or nonstick liner.

2 Combine flour, coconut, almonds, sugar, baking powder and salt in bowl of electric stand mixer.

3 Lightly beat together egg, egg white, butter and vanilla in mixing bowl. With mixer speed on low, add egg mixture to dry ingredients. Blend together.

4 Divide dough into 2 equal pieces. Dust your hands lightly with flour and shape each piece of dough into a loaf about 8 inches long, 2 to 3 inches wide and ¾ inch high. Place loaves on baking sheet, leaving several inches between them.

5 Bake loaves 26 to 28 minutes until golden and set. Cool on wire rack 10 minutes. Slice each loaf into ½-inch-thick slices. Place slices on their sides on baking sheets. Bake 20 minutes or until firm and golden. Remove from oven and cool on rack.

CUTTING BISCOTTI

When cutting biscotti, use a sharp serrated knife and cut on the diagonal. The cookies will be the perfect size for dunking in coffee, milk, or wine.

CHOCOLATE CHIP COOKIES

MAKES ABOUT 54 COOKIES

1 **cup granulated sugar**
1 **cup packed brown sugar**
1 **cup (2 sticks) butter, softened**
2 **eggs**
1½ **teaspoons vanilla**
1 **teaspoon baking soda**
1 **teaspoon salt**
3 **cups all-purpose flour**
12 **ounces semisweet chocolate chips**

1 Preheat oven to 375°F. Grease baking sheets. Place sugars, butter, eggs and vanilla in bowl of electric stand mixer. Mix on low speed 30 seconds. Stop and scrape bowl. Turn to medium-low and beat about 30 seconds. Stop and scrape bowl.

2 Turn to low. Gradually add baking soda, salt and flour to sugar mixture and mix about 2 minutes. Stop and scrape bowl. Add chocolate chips. Mix about 15 seconds more.

3 Drop dough by rounded teaspoonfuls onto prepared baking sheets about 2 inches apart. Bake 10 to 12 minutes. Remove from baking sheets immediately and cool on wire racks.

![Stack of oatmeal cookies]

OLD-FASHIONED OATMEAL COOKIES

MAKES 36 COOKIES

1 Preheat oven to 350°F. Line cookie sheets with parchment paper.

2 Combine oats, flour, baking soda, baking powder and salt in medium bowl. Beat brown sugar, butter and granulated sugar in bowl of electric stand mixer at medium speed until light and fluffy. Add egg, honey and vanilla; beat until well blended. Gradually add flour mixture, about ½ cup at a time; beat just until blended. Drop dough by tablespoonfuls about 2 inches apart on prepared cookie sheets.

3 Bake 11 to 15 minutes or until cookies are puffed and golden. Do not overbake. Cool 5 minutes on cookie sheets. Remove to wire racks to cool completely.

- 2 cups old-fashioned oats
- 1⅓ cups all-purpose flour
- ¾ teaspoon baking soda
- ½ teaspoon baking powder
- ½ teaspoon salt
- 1 cup packed light brown sugar
- ¾ cup (1½ sticks) butter, softened
- ¼ cup granulated sugar
- 1 egg
- 1 tablespoon honey
- 1 teaspoon vanilla

LEMON DROPS

MAKES ABOUT 72 COOKIES

- **2 cups all-purpose flour**
- **⅛ teaspoon salt**
- **1 cup (2 sticks) butter, softened**
- **1 cup powdered sugar, divided**
- **Grated peel of 1 large lemon**
- **2 teaspoons lemon juice**

1 Preheat oven to 300°F.

2 Combine flour and salt in medium bowl. Beat butter and ¾ cup powdered sugar in bowl of electric stand mixer at medium speed until fluffy. Beat in lemon peel and juice. Add flour mixture, ½ cup at a time, beating just until blended after each addition.

3 Shape dough by rounded teaspoonfuls into balls. Place 1 inch apart on ungreased cookie sheets. Bake 20 to 25 minutes or until cookies are lightly browned on bottom. Cool on cookie sheets 5 minutes. Remove to wire racks; cool completely. Sprinkle with remaining ¼ cup powdered sugar.

CARROT CAKE COOKIES

MAKES ABOUT 36 COOKIES

1 Preheat oven to 350°F. Grease cookie sheets.

2 Fit processor with steel blade. Grate carrots; set aside. Combine flour, cinnamon, baking soda and salt in medium bowl. Beat brown sugar and butter in bowl of electric stand mixer at medium speed until creamy. Add egg and vanilla; beat until well blended. Beat in flour mixture. Stir in carrots, walnuts and raisins, if desired. Drop dough by rounded tablespoonfuls 2 inches apart onto prepared cookie sheets.

3 Bake 12 to 14 minutes or until set and edges are lightly browned. Cool on cookie sheets 1 minute. Remove to wire racks; cool completely.

- **2 medium carrots**
- **1½ cups all-purpose flour**
- **1 teaspoon ground cinnamon**
- **½ teaspoon baking soda**
- **½ teaspoon salt**
- **¾ cup packed brown sugar**
- **½ cup (1 stick) butter, softened**
- **1 egg**
- **½ teaspoon vanilla**
- **½ cup chopped walnuts**
- **½ cup raisins or chopped dried pineapple (optional)**

EXTRA-CHOCOLATEY BROWNIE COOKIES

MAKES 36 COOKIES

- 2 **cups all-purpose flour**
- ½ **cup unsweetened Dutch process cocoa powder**
- 1 **teaspoon baking soda**
- ¾ **teaspoon salt**
- 1 **cup (2 sticks) butter, softened**
- 1 **cup packed brown sugar**
- ½ **cup granulated sugar**
- 2 **eggs**
- 2 **teaspoons vanilla**
- 1 **package (11½ ounces) semisweet chocolate chunks**
- 2 **cups coarsely chopped walnuts or pecans**

1 Preheat oven to 375°F. Whisk flour, cocoa, baking soda and salt in medium bowl until well blended.

2 Beat butter in bowl of electric stand mixer at medium speed 1 minute or until light and fluffy. Add brown sugar and granulated sugar; beat 2 minutes or until fluffy. Add eggs and vanilla; beat until well blended. Add flour mixture; beat at low speed until blended. Stir in chocolate chunks and walnuts.

3 Drop dough by heaping tablespoonfuls 2 inches apart onto ungreased cookie sheets; flatten slightly.

4 Bake 12 minutes or until set. Cool on cookie sheets 2 minutes. Remove to wire racks; cool completely. Store in airtight container at room temperature up to 4 days.

SOFT GINGER COOKIES

MAKES ABOUT 30 COOKIES

1 Preheat oven to 350°F.

2 Combine flour, ginger, baking soda, salt, cinnamon and cloves in large bowl. Beat brown sugar, oil and molasses in bowl of electric stand mixer at medium speed 1 minute until smooth. Add sour cream and egg white; beat until well blended. Gradually add flour mixture, beating at low speed until well blended.

3 Drop dough by rounded tablespoonfuls 2 inches apart onto ungreased cookie sheets. Flatten dough to ⅛-inch thickness with bottom of glass lightly sprayed with nonstick cooking spray.

4 Bake 10 minutes or until tops of cookies puff up and spring back when lightly touched. Cool 2 minutes on cookie sheets. Remove to wire racks; cool completely.

2	cups all-purpose flour
1½	teaspoons ground ginger
1	teaspoon baking soda
¼	teaspoon salt
¼	teaspoon ground cinnamon
¼	teaspoon ground cloves
¼	cup packed light brown sugar
¼	cup canola oil
¼	cup molasses
½	cup fat-free sour cream
1	egg white

PEANUT BUTTER COOKIES

MAKES 36 COOKIES

½ **cup peanut butter**
½ **cup butter, softened**
½ **cup granulated sugar**
½ **cup packed brown sugar**
1 **egg**
½ **teaspoon vanilla**
½ **teaspoon baking soda**
¼ **teaspoon salt**
1¼ **cups all-purpose flour**

1 Preheat oven to 375°F. Place peanut butter and butter in bowl of electric stand mixer. Attach flat beater to mixer. Turn to medium and beat until mixture is smooth, about 1 minute. Stop and scrape bowl. Add granulated sugar, brown sugar, egg and vanilla. Turn to medium-low and beat about 1 minute. Stop and scrape bowl.

2 Turn to low. Gradually add all remaining ingredients to sugar mixture and mix about 30 seconds.

3 Roll dough into 1-inch balls. Place about 2 inches apart on ungreased baking sheets. Press flat with fork in a criss-cross pattern to ¼-inch thickness.

4 Bake 10 to 12 minutes until golden brown. Remove from baking sheets immediately and cool on wire racks.

GINGERY OAT AND MOLASSES COOKIES

MAKES ABOUT 48 COOKIES

1 Combine all-purpose flour, whole wheat flour, oats, baking powder, ground ginger, baking soda, cinnamon and salt in medium bowl.

2 Beat sugar and butter in bowl of electric stand mixer at high speed until light and fluffy. Beat in egg, molasses and vanilla. Gradually beat in flour mixture. Stir in crystallized ginger and walnuts. Shape into 2 logs about 8 to 10 inches long. Wrap and refrigerate 1 to 3 hours.

3 Preheat oven to 350°F. Grease cookie sheets. Cut logs into ⅓-inch slices. Place 1½ inches apart on prepared cookie sheets. Bake 12 to 14 minutes or until set and browned at edges. Cool on cookie sheets 5 minutes. Remove to wire racks; cool completely.

- 1 **cup all-purpose flour**
- ¾ **cup whole wheat flour**
- ½ **cup old-fashioned oats**
- 1½ **teaspoons baking powder**
- 1½ **teaspoons ground ginger**
- 1 **teaspoon baking soda**
- ½ **teaspoon ground cinnamon**
- ¼ **teaspoon salt**
- ¾ **cup sugar**
- ½ **cup (1 stick) unsalted butter, softened**
- 1 **egg**
- ¼ **cup molasses**
- ¼ **teaspoon vanilla**
- 1 **cup chopped crystallized ginger***
- ½ **cup chopped walnuts**

Crystallized ginger can be found in the baking aisle or the Asian food section of most supermarkets.

PECAN SHORTBREAD COOKIES

MAKES 24 COOKIES

1 cup (2 sticks) butter
1 teaspoon vanilla
¾ cup packed brown sugar
2½ cups all-purpose flour
½ cup chopped pecans

TIP

Store crisp cookies in an airtight container with a loose-fitting lid. If they soften, place them in an oven at 300°F for 3 to 5 minutes before serving.

Soft cookies should be stored between layers of waxed paper in an airtight container. A piece of apple or bread, changed frequently, will help keep cookies soft.

1 Place butter, vanilla and brown sugar in bowl of electric stand mixer. Beat at medium-high 1 minute. Stop and scrape bowl.

2 Turn to medium-low and add flour; beat 30 seconds. Stop and scrape bowl. Turn to low and add pecans, mixing just until blended. Shape dough into a log 1½ inches in diameter. Wrap in waxed paper and chill 20 minutes.

3 Preheat oven to 325°F. Slice dough into ½-inch-thick cookies. Place on greased baking sheets. Bake for 18 to 20 minutes. Cool on wire racks.

PB & J THUMBPRINT COOKIES
MAKES ABOUT 40 COOKIES

1 Preheat oven to 350°F. Line cookie sheets with parchment paper.

2 Combine oats, flour, baking soda, baking powder and salt in medium bowl. Beat brown sugar, butter and granulated sugar in bowl of electric stand mixer at medium speed until well blended. Beat at high speed until light and fluffy. Add peanut butter, egg, honey and vanilla; beat at medium speed until well blended. Gradually add flour mixture; beat just until blended. Stir in peanuts. Drop dough by rounded tablespoonfuls onto prepared cookie sheets.

3 Bake 10 minutes. Remove cookies from oven. Press center of each cookie with back of teaspoon to make a slight indentation; fill with about ½ teaspoon jelly. Return to oven; bake 4 to 6 minutes or until puffed and golden. Cool 5 minutes on cookie sheets; remove to wire racks to cool completely.

2 cups old-fashioned oats

1⅓ cups plus 1 tablespoon all-purpose flour

¾ teaspoon baking soda

½ teaspoon baking powder

½ teaspoon salt

1 cup packed brown sugar

¾ cup (1½ sticks) butter, softened

¼ cup granulated sugar

¼ cup chunky peanut butter

1 egg

1 tablespoon honey

1 teaspoon vanilla

½ cup chopped peanuts, unsalted or honey-roasted

½ cup grape jelly or flavor of choice

MUFFINS

How could a warm buttered muffin not be the perfect start to any day?

SPICY SWEET POTATO MUFFINS

MAKES 12 MUFFINS

⅓ cup plus 2 tablespoons packed brown sugar, divided

2 teaspoons ground cinnamon, divided

1½ cups all-purpose flour

2 teaspoons baking powder

½ teaspoon salt

½ teaspoon baking soda

½ teaspoon ground allspice

1 cup mashed cooked or canned sweet potatoes

¾ cup buttermilk

¼ cup vegetable oil

1 egg, beaten

1 Preheat oven to 425°F. Grease 12 standard (2½-inch) muffin cups or line with paper baking cups.

2 Combine 2 tablespoons brown sugar and 1 teaspoon cinnamon in small bowl; set aside.

3 Sift flour, baking powder, remaining 1 teaspoon cinnamon, salt, baking soda and allspice into bowl of electric stand mixer. Stir in remaining ⅓ cup brown sugar.

4 Combine sweet potatoes, buttermilk, oil and egg in medium bowl. With mixer on low, stir buttermilk mixture into dry ingredients just until moistened. Spoon batter into prepared muffin cups, filling each two-thirds full. Sprinkle each muffin with ½ teaspoon cinnamon mixture. Bake 14 to 16 minutes or until toothpick inserted into centers comes out clean.

STREUSEL-TOPPED BLUEBERRY MUFFINS

MAKES 12 MUFFINS

1½ cups plus ⅓ cup all-purpose flour, divided

½ cup plus ⅓ cup sugar, divided

1 teaspoon ground cinnamon

3 tablespoons cold butter, cut into small pieces

2 teaspoons baking powder

½ teaspoon salt

1 cup milk

¼ cup butter, melted and slightly cooled

1 egg, beaten

1 teaspoon vanilla

1 cup fresh blueberries

1 Preheat oven to 375°F. Grease 12 standard (2½-inch) muffin cups or line with paper baking cups.

2 Combine ⅓ cup flour, ⅓ cup sugar and cinnamon in small bowl. Cut in 3 tablespoons butter with pastry blender until mixture resembles coarse crumbs; set aside.

3 Combine remaining 1½ cups flour, ½ cup sugar, baking powder and salt in bowl of electric stand mixer. Combine milk, ¼ cup melted butter, egg and vanilla in small bowl. With mixer on low, stir milk mixture into flour mixture just until moistened. Fold in blueberries. Spoon evenly into prepared muffin cups. Sprinkle reserved topping over top of each muffin.

4 Bake 20 to 25 minutes or until toothpick inserted into centers comes out clean. Remove from pan; cool completely.

WHAT'S A PASTRY BLENDER?

A pastry blender is a handheld tool with several u-shaped wires that connect to a straight handle. The u-shaped wires cut ingredients together with ease, and since the pastry cutter stays cool, it keeps the butter or shortening at an optimum temperature.

SUN-DRIED TOMATO-BASIL MUFFINS

MAKES 12 MUFFINS

½ **cup sun-dried tomatoes (not packed in oil)**

2 **cups all-purpose flour**

1 **tablespoon baking powder**

1½ **tablespoons finely chopped fresh basil**

½ **teaspoon salt**

¼ **teaspoon black pepper**

⅛ **teaspoon garlic powder**

¾ **cup fat-free (skim) milk**

½ **cup (4 ounces) low-fat (1%) cottage cheese**

1 **egg**

3 **tablespoons canola oil**

2 **teaspoons minced dried onion**

1 Preheat oven to 400°F. Spray 12 standard (2½-inch) muffin cups with nonstick cooking spray or line with foil baking cups. Cover tomatoes with hot water in small bowl; let stand 10 minutes. Drain; finely chop.

2 Combine flour, baking powder, basil, salt, pepper and garlic powder in bowl of electric stand mixer. Combine milk, cottage cheese, egg, oil, onion and tomatoes in medium bowl. With mixer on low, add milk mixture to flour mixture, mixing just until combined.

3 Spoon batter into prepared muffin cups. Bake 20 to 25 minutes or until toothpick inserted in center comes out clean. Cool in pan 5 minutes. Serve warm.

BAKING WITH HERBS

Fresh herbs can give your baked goods a nice, bright flavor, but they're not always readily available. To substitute dried herbs for fresh, use 1 part dried for 3 parts fresh herbs. For this recipe, you would use 1½ teaspoons dried basil instead of the 1 tablespoon fresh.

PEANUT BUTTER BRAN MUFFINS

MAKES 12 MUFFINS

½ **cup peanut butter**
2 **tablespoons butter**
¼ **cup packed brown sugar**
1 **large egg**
1 **cup whole bran cereal**
1 **cup milk**
¾ **cup all-purpose flour**
1 **tablespoon baking powder**
½ **teaspoon salt**
½ **cup dark raisins**

1 Preheat oven to 400°F. Fit food processor with steel blade. Measure peanut butter, butter, sugar and egg into work bowl. Process until smooth, 5 to 10 seconds. Add cereal and milk; process on/off just until blended.

2 Add flour, baking powder and salt to cereal mixture. Process on/off 2 or 3 times, or just until flour is moistened. Do not overprocess. Batter should be lumpy. Sprinkle raisins over batter. Process on/off just until raisins are mixed into batter.

3 Spoon batter into greased muffin cups, filling each about three-fourths full. Bake until golden, 20 to 25 minutes. Serve warm.

WHICH MILK WHEN?

Many baking recipes call for milk. While some will specify precisely which type of milk to use, many will not. For the most part, using whole milk in baking is ideal. But you can certainly substitute 1% or 2% milk in most cases without compromising taste or texture.

WILD RICE MUFFINS

MAKES 12 MUFFINS

½ cup all-purpose flour

½ cup whole wheat flour

1½ teaspoons baking powder

1 teaspoon baking soda

¼ teaspoon salt

¼ teaspoon ground cinnamon

⅓ cup packed dark brown sugar

¼ cup (½ stick) unsalted butter, at room temperature

1 egg

½ to ⅔ cup reduced-fat (2%) milk

1 cup cooked wild rice

½ cup coarsely chopped pecans

½ cup pitted chopped dates

1 Preheat oven to 400°F. Grease 12 standard (2½-inch) muffin cups or line with paper baking cups. Combine flours, baking powder, baking soda, salt and cinnamon in medium bowl and mix well.

2 Cream brown sugar and butter in bowl of electric stand mixer at high speed. Add egg; beat well. Add ½ cup milk; beat well. Scrape down bowl. Add wild rice; mix at low speed. Add flour mixture to batter, half at a time. Beat at medium speed, just until flour is mixed in. (Do not overmix.) Batter should be somewhat wet; if batter is stiff, add remaining milk, 1 tablespoon at a time. Stir in pecans and dates by hand.

3 Spoon batter into prepared muffin cups, filling two-thirds to three-quarters full. Bake 12 to 15 minutes or until toothpick inserted into centers comes out clean. Remove from oven. Cool 2 minutes in pan. Transfer to wire rack to cool completely.

DATES ARE GREAT

Dates are a delicious and nutritious way to add sweetness to baked goods, especially muffins and quick breads. They are naturally sweet and have a flavor very similar to honey. Plus, they are high in calcium, potassium and iron.

CHERRY-LEMON POPPY SEED MUFFINS

MAKES 12 MUFFINS

2 cups all-purpose flour

1 cup sugar

1 tablespoon baking powder

1 teaspoon salt

¾ cup buttermilk

¼ cup vegetable oil

¼ cup (½ stick) unsalted
    butter, melted

2 eggs, lightly beaten
    Grated peel of 1 lemon

1 tablespoon fresh lemon
    juice

1 teaspoon vanilla

½ cup dried cherries, chopped

½ cup chopped pecans

2 tablespoons poppy seeds

1 Preheat oven to 350°F. Grease 12 standard (2½-inch) muffin cups or line with paper baking cups.

2 Combine flour, sugar, baking powder and salt in bowl of electric stand mixer.

3 Combine buttermilk, oil, butter, eggs, lemon peel, lemon juice and vanilla in medium bowl. Pour into flour mixture; stir just until blended. Stir in cherries, pecans and poppy seeds just until blended. Spoon batter evenly into prepared muffin cups.

4 Bake 20 to 24 minutes or until golden brown and toothpick inserted into centers comes out clean. Cool in pan 5 minutes. Remove to wire rack; cool completely. Store in airtight container.

GRATING LEMON PEEL

Freshly grated lemon peel adds an extra pop of flavor to many dishes. You can use a standard grater or a zester, but be careful to grate only the bright yellow part of the peel. If you grate too deep, you'll include the bitter white pith.

GINGER SQUASH MUFFINS

MAKES 12 MUFFINS

1½ **cups all-purpose flour**

⅓ **cup whole wheat flour**

⅓ **cup granulated sugar**

¼ **cup packed dark brown sugar**

2½ **teaspoons baking powder**

1 **teaspoon ground cinnamon**

½ **teaspoon baking soda**

½ **teaspoon salt**

½ **teaspoon ground ginger**

1 **cup frozen winter squash, thawed***

2 **eggs, beaten**

⅓ **cup canola oil**

¼ **cup finely chopped walnuts**

2 **tablespoons finely chopped crystallized ginger (optional)**

*One 12-ounce package frozen squash yields about 1 cup squash. Or, use puréed cooked fresh butternut squash.

1 Preheat oven to 375°F. Spray 12 standard (2½-inch) muffin cups with nonstick cooking spray.

2 Combine all-purpose flour, whole wheat flour, granulated sugar, brown sugar, baking powder, cinnamon, baking soda, salt and ground ginger in bowl of electric stand mixer; mix well.

3 Combine squash, eggs and oil in small bowl until well blended. Add to flour mixture; mix on low just until blended. (Do not overmix.) Stir in walnuts and crystallized ginger, if desired. Spoon batter into prepared muffin cups, filling two-thirds full.

4 Bake 18 to 20 minutes or until toothpick inserted into centers comes out clean. Cool in pan 5 minutes. Remove to wire rack; cool completely.

JALAPEÑO CORN MUFFINS

MAKES 18 MUFFINS

1½ cups yellow cornmeal

¾ cup all-purpose flour

2 teaspoons baking powder

½ teaspoon baking soda

½ teaspoon salt

2 eggs

4 tablespoons (½ stick) butter, melted and cooled

2 tablespoons sugar

¾ cup buttermilk

1 can (8 ounces) cream-style corn

1 cup Monterey Jack or Cheddar cheese

2 fresh jalapeño peppers,* seeded and finely chopped

Jalapeño peppers can sting and irritate the skin, so wear rubber gloves when handling peppers and do not touch your eyes.

1 Preheat oven to 400°F. Grease 18 standard (2½-inch) muffin cups or line with paper baking cups.

2 Place cornmeal, flour, baking powder, baking soda and salt in bowl of electric stand mixer. Mix at low speed until combined. In separate bowl, whisk eggs, butter and sugar. Add buttermilk; mix gently.

3 Add egg mixture to flour mixture; beat at medium speed until combined. Add corn, cheese and peppers to batter. Mix at low speed until combined; do not overbeat.

4 Fill prepared muffin cups three-fourths full. Bake 15 to 17 minutes or until muffins are golden brown. Let cool 5 minutes before serving.

LEMON POPPY SEED MUFFINS

MAKES 18 MUFFINS

1 Preheat oven to 400°F. Grease 18 standard (2½-inch) muffin cups or line with paper baking cups.

2 Combine flour, granulated sugar, poppy seeds, 2 tablespoons lemon peel, baking powder, baking soda, cardamom and salt in bowl of electric stand mixer. Beat eggs in medium bowl. Add butter, milk and ½ cup lemon juice; mix well. Add egg mixture to flour mixture; stir just until blended. Spoon batter evenly into prepared muffin cups, filling three-fourths full.

3 Bake 15 to 20 minutes or until toothpick inserted into centers comes out clean. Cool in pans on wire racks 10 minutes.

4 Meanwhile, prepare glaze. Combine powdered sugar and remaining 2 teaspoons lemon peel in small bowl; stir in enough remaining lemon juice to make pourable glaze. Drizzle glaze over muffins. Serve warm or at room temperature.

- **2 cups all-purpose flour**
- **1¼ cups granulated sugar**
- **¼ cup poppy seeds**
- **2 tablespoons plus 2 teaspoons grated lemon peel, divided**
- **2 teaspoons baking powder**
- **½ teaspoon baking soda**
- **½ teaspoon ground cardamom**
- **¼ teaspoon salt**
- **2 eggs**
- **½ cup (1 stick) butter, melted**
- **½ cup milk**
- **½ cup plus 2 tablespoons lemon juice, divided**
- **1 cup powdered sugar**

DOUBLE CHOCOLATE ZUCCHINI MUFFINS

MAKES 12 JUMBO MUFFINS

2⅓ cups all-purpose flour

1¼ cups sugar

⅓ cup unsweetened cocoa powder

2 teaspoons baking powder

1½ teaspoons ground cinnamon

1 teaspoon baking soda

½ teaspoon salt

1 cup sour cream

½ cup vegetable oil

2 eggs, beaten

¼ cup milk

1 cup milk chocolate chips

1 cup shredded zucchini

1 Preheat oven to 400°F. Grease 12 jumbo (3½-inch) muffin cups or line with paper baking cups.

2 Place flour, sugar, cocoa, baking powder, cinnamon, baking soda and salt in bowl of electric stand mixer; mix at low speed 30 seconds. Combine sour cream, oil, eggs and milk in medium bowl until blended; add to flour mixture. Mix at low speed just until moistened. Fold in chocolate chips and zucchini. Spoon batter into prepared muffin cups, filling half full.

3 Bake 25 to 30 minutes or until toothpick inserted into centers comes out clean. Serve warm.

Variation: For standard-size muffins, spoon batter into 18 standard (2½-inch) paper-lined or greased muffin cups. Bake at 400°F for 18 to 20 minutes or until toothpick inserted into centers comes out clean.

BOSTON BROWN BREAD MUFFINS

MAKES 12 MUFFINS

1 Preheat oven to 400°F. Grease 12 standard (2½-inch) muffin cups or line with paper baking cups.

2 Place flours, cornmeal, baking soda and salt in bowl of electric stand mixer. Mix at low speed 30 seconds or until combined. Combine buttermilk, sugar, molasses, beer and egg in medium bowl. Add to flour mixture along with raisins; mix at low speed until combined. Fill prepared muffin cups three-fourths full.

3 Bake 15 minutes or until toothpick inserted into centers comes out clean. Serve with cream cheese.

½ cup rye flour
½ cup whole wheat flour
½ cup yellow cornmeal
1½ teaspoons baking soda
¾ teaspoon salt
1 cup buttermilk
⅓ cup packed dark brown sugar
⅓ cup molasses
⅓ cup dark beer
1 egg
1 cup golden raisins
Cream cheese, softened

RASPBERRY CORN MUFFINS

MAKES 12 MUFFINS

1 cup all-purpose flour

¾ cup cornmeal

2 teaspoons baking powder

½ teaspoon baking soda

¼ teaspoon salt

1 egg, beaten

1 cup reduced-fat sour cream

⅓ cup thawed frozen unsweetened apple juice concentrate

1½ cups fresh or frozen raspberries

⅔ cup reduced-fat whipped cream cheese

2 tablespoons raspberry fruit spread

1 Preheat oven to 350°F. Spray 12 standard (2½-inch) muffin cups with nonstick cooking spray.

2 Combine flour, cornmeal, baking powder, baking soda and salt in bowl of electric stand mixer. Whisk together egg, sour cream and apple juice concentrate in medium bowl. Add egg mixture to flour mixture; stir just until moistened. Do not overmix. Gently stir in raspberries.

3 Spoon batter into prepared muffin cups, filling three-fourths full. Bake 18 to 20 minutes or until golden brown. Let stand in pan on wire rack 5 minutes. Remove from pan; cool slightly.

4 Combine cream cheese and fruit spread in small serving bowl. Serve with warm muffins.

CRANBERRY CHOCOLATE-CHUNK MUFFINS

MAKES 12 MUFFINS

1 Preheat oven to 350°F. Grease 12 standard (2½-inch) muffin cups or line with paper liners. Combine flour, sugar, baking powder and salt in bowl of electric stand mixer. Add milk, oil, eggs and vanilla; mix on low until combined. Add pecans, chocolate and dried cranberries; mix well. Divide batter evenly among muffin cups.

2 Bake 15 minutes or until light golden brown. Cool in pans 5 minutes. Remove to wire rack; cool completely.

2 cups all-purpose flour
½ cup granulated sugar
2 teaspoons baking powder
½ teaspoon salt
½ cup milk
½ cup vegetable oil
2 eggs
1 teaspoon vanilla
¾ cup coarsely chopped pecans*
1 (4-ounce) semisweet chocolate bar, chopped into ½-inch chunks (about ¾ cup)
½ cup coarsely chopped dried cranberries

*For more flavor, toast pecans; spread in single layer in heavy-bottomed skillet. Cook over medium heat 1 to 2 minutes, stirring frequently, until pecans are lightly browned. Remove from skillet immediately. Cool before using.

PUMPKIN CHOCOLATE CHIP MUFFINS

MAKES 18 MUFFINS

2½ **cups all-purpose flour**

1 **tablespoon baking powder**

1½ **teaspoons pumpkin pie spice***

½ **teaspoon salt**

1 **cup solid-pack pumpkin**

1 **cup packed light brown sugar**

¾ **cup milk**

6 **tablespoons butter, melted**

2 **eggs**

1 **cup semisweet chocolate chips**

½ **cup chopped walnuts**

*Or substitute ¾ teaspoon ground cinnamon, ⅜ teaspoon ground ginger and scant ¼ teaspoon each ground allspice and ground nutmeg.

1 Preheat oven to 400°F. Grease 18 standard (2½-inch) muffin cups or line with paper baking cups.

2 Combine flour, baking powder, pumpkin pie spice and salt in bowl of electric stand mixer. Beat pumpkin, sugar, milk, butter and eggs in medium bowl until well blended. Add pumpkin mixture, chocolate chips and walnuts to flour mixture; mix at low speed 30 seconds or just until moistened. Spoon evenly into prepared muffin cups, filling two-thirds full.

3 Bake 15 to 17 minutes or until toothpick inserted into centers comes out clean. Cool in pans on wire racks 10 minutes. Remove from pans to racks; cool completely.

TOFFEE CRUNCH MUFFINS

MAKES 36 MINI MUFFINS

1 Preheat oven to 400°F. Grease 36 mini (1¾-inch) muffin cups or line with paper baking cups.

2 Combine flour, sugar, baking powder, baking soda and salt in bowl of electric stand mixer. Combine milk, sour cream, egg, butter and vanilla in small bowl until well blended. Stir into flour mixture until moistened. Fold in two thirds of toffee. Spoon batter into prepared muffin cups. Sprinkle evenly with remaining toffee.

3 Bake 16 to 18 minutes or until toothpick inserted into centers comes out clean. Remove from pans; cool on wire racks 10 minutes. Serve warm or at room temperature.

Variation: For larger muffins, spoon batter into 10 standard (2½-inch) greased or paper-lined muffin cups. Bake at 350°F for about 20 minutes or until toothpick inserted into centers comes out clean. Makes 10 muffins.

1½ **cups all-purpose flour**
⅓ **cup packed brown sugar**
2 **teaspoons baking powder**
½ **teaspoon baking soda**
½ **teaspoon salt**
½ **cup milk**
½ **cup sour cream**
1 **egg, beaten**
3 **tablespoons butter, melted**
1 **teaspoon vanilla**
3 **bars (1.4 ounces each) chocolate-covered toffee, chopped, divided**

PIES & TARTS

Flaky crust plus luscious filling is just about as good as it gets

SOUR CREAM SQUASH PIE

MAKES 8 SERVINGS

Graham Cracker Crumb Crust (recipe follows)
1 **package (12 ounces) frozen winter squash, thawed and excess water drained**
½ **cup sour cream**
¼ **cup sugar**
1 **egg**
1½ **teaspoons pumpkin pie spice**
½ **teaspoon salt**
½ **teaspoon vanilla**
¾ **cup evaporated milk**
¼ **cup chopped hazelnuts, toasted**

1 Preheat oven to 350°F. Prepare Graham Cracker Crumb Crust.

2 Whisk squash, sour cream, sugar, egg, pumpkin pie spice, salt and vanilla in bowl of electric stand mixer until blended. Beat in milk. Pour into crust.

3 Bake 1 hour and 10 minutes or until set. Cool completely; sprinkle with hazelnuts just before serving.

GRAHAM CRACKER CRUMB CRUST

22 **to 24 square graham crackers, broken into pieces**
⅓ **cup sugar**
¼ **to ⅓ cup butter, melted**

Preheat oven to 350°F. Place crackers in food processor. Process using on/off pulses until finely crushed. Combine crumbs, sugar and butter in medium bowl; mix well. Press firmly onto bottom and up side of 9-inch pie plate. Bake about 8 minutes or until browned. Cool completely.

PIE PASTRY

MAKES 2 (8- OR 9-INCH) CRUSTS

2¼ **cups all-purpose flour**
¾ **teaspoon salt**
½ **cup cold shortening**
2 **tablespoons cold butter**
5 **to 6 tablespoons cold water**

ROLLING OUT PIE DOUGH

Rolling out pie dough can be tricky. Position the rolling pin in the center of the dough and roll away from you. Reposition the pin in the center of the dough and roll towards you. Always use even pressure and roll from the center of the dough.

1 Place flour and salt in bowl of electric stand mixer. Turn to low speed and mix about 15 seconds. Cut shortening and butter into pieces and add to flour mixture. Turn to low and mix until shortening particles are size of small peas, 30 to 45 seconds.

2 Continuing on low speed, add water, 1 tablespoon at a time, mixing until ingredients are moistened and dough begins to hold together. Divide dough in half. Pat each half into smooth ball and flatten slightly. Wrap in plastic wrap. Chill in refrigerator 15 minutes.

3 Roll one half of dough to ⅛-inch thickness between sheets of waxed paper. Fold pastry into quarters. Ease into 8- or 9-inch pie plate and unfold, pressing firmly against bottom and sides.

For One-Crust Pie: Fold edge under. Crimp as desired. Add desired pie filling. Bake as directed.

For Two-Crust Pie: Trim pastry even with edge of pie plate. Using second half of dough, roll out another pastry crust. Add desired pie filling. Top with second pastry crust. Seal edge. Crimp as desired. Cut slits for steam to escape. Bake as directed.

For Baked Pastry Shell: Fold edge under. Crimp as desired. Prick sides and bottom with fork. Bake at 450°F for 8 to 10 minutes or until lightly browned. Cool completely on wire rack and fill.

Alternate Method for Baked Pastry Shell: Fold edge under. Crimp as desired. Line shell with foil. Fill with pie weights or dried beans. Bake at 450°F for 10 to 12 minutes, or until edges are lightly browned. Remove pie weights and foil. Cool completely on wire rack and fill.

CHOCOLATE PECAN PIE

MAKES 8 SERVINGS

1 Preheat oven to 350°F. Prepare Pie Pastry.

2 Beat eggs, sugar and corn syrup in bowl of electric stand mixer at medium-high speed 1 minute. Stop and scrape bowl.

3 Turn mixer to medium speed and gradually add chocolate; beat 1 minute until well blended. Stir in pecans. Pour mixture into pie shell. Bake 35 to 45 minutes or until almost set.

1 **unbaked Pie Pastry for One-Crust Pie (page 116)**

4 **eggs**

1 **cup sugar**

1 **cup dark corn syrup**

3 **squares (1 ounce each) unsweetened chocolate, melted**

2 **cups pecan halves**

DEEP-DISH STREUSEL PEACH PIE

MAKES ABOUT 6 SERVINGS

- **1 can (29 ounces) or 2 cans (16 ounces each) cling peach slices in syrup**
- **⅓ cup plus 1 tablespoon granulated sugar, divided**
- **1 tablespoon cornstarch**
- **½ teaspoon vanilla**
- **½ cup packed brown sugar**
- **2 cups all-purpose flour, divided**
- **⅓ cup quick oats**
- **¼ cup (½ stick) butter, melted**
- **½ teaspoon ground cinnamon**
- **½ teaspoon salt**
- **½ cup shortening**
- **4 to 5 tablespoons cold water**
  Sweetened Whipped Cream (recipe follows)

1 Preheat oven to 350°F. Drain peach slices, reserving ¾ cup syrup. Combine ⅓ cup granulated sugar and cornstarch in small saucepan. Gradually add reserved syrup; stir until well blended. Cook and stir over low heat until thickened. Remove from heat; stir in vanilla. Set aside.

2 Combine brown sugar, ½ cup flour, oats, butter and cinnamon in small bowl; stir until mixture forms coarse crumbs. Set aside.

3 Combine remaining 1½ cups flour, remaining 1 tablespoon granulated sugar and salt in small bowl. Cut in shortening until mixture forms pea-sized crumbs. Sprinkle water, 1 tablespoon at a time, over flour mixture. Toss lightly with fork until mixture holds together. Press together to form a ball. Shape into 5- to 6-inch disc. Roll dough into ⅛-inch-thick square on lightly floured surface. Trim into 10-inch square. Press dough onto bottom and 1 inch up sides of 8-inch square baking dish. Arrange peaches over crust. Pour sauce over peaches. Sprinkle with crumb topping. Bake 45 minutes.

4 Prepare Sweetened Whipped Cream. Serve pie warm or at room temperature with Sweetened Whipped Cream.

SWEETENED WHIPPED CREAM

- **1 cup cold whipping cream**
- **3 tablespoons sugar**
- **½ teaspoon vanilla**

Chill mixer bowl and wire whip. Beat cream in mixer bowl at high speed until soft peaks form. Gradually add sugar and vanilla. Whip until stiff peaks form.

ITALIAN CHOCOLATE PIE

MAKES 8 SERVINGS

¼ **cup pine nuts**

3 **tablespoons packed brown sugar**

1 **tablespoon grated orange peel**

1 **unbaked Pie Pastry for One-Crust Pie (page 116)**

4 **ounces bittersweet chocolate, coarsely chopped**

3 **tablespoons unsalted butter**

1 **can (5 ounces) evaporated milk**

3 **eggs**

3 **tablespoons hazelnut liqueur**

1 **teaspoon vanilla**
   Whipped cream (optional)
   Chocolate curls (optional)

1 Toast pine nuts in dry nonstick skillet over medium heat, stirring constantly until golden brown and aromatic. Remove from heat. Finely chop; cool. Combine pine nuts, brown sugar and orange peel in small bowl. Sprinkle onto bottom of pie crust; gently press into crust.

2 Preheat oven to 325°F. Melt chocolate and butter in small saucepan over low heat, stirring constantly until blended and smooth. Let cool to room temperature.

3 Beat chocolate mixture and evaporated milk in bowl of electric stand mixer at medium speed. Add eggs, one at a time, beating well after each addition. Stir in hazelnut liqueur and vanilla. Pour into pie crust.

4 Bake on center rack of oven 30 to 40 minutes or until filling is set. Cool completely on wire rack. Refrigerate until ready to serve. Serve with whipped cream and chocolate curls, if desired.

MAKING CHOCOLATE CURLS

To make chocolate curls, run a vegetable peeler gently down a block of chocolate to skim off a small layer. Place curls on piece of parchment paper and refrigerate until ready to use.

LEMON MERINGUE PIE

MAKES 8 SERVINGS

FILLING

- **1 cup sugar**
- **1½ cups water**
- **¼ teaspoon salt**
- **⅓ cup cornstarch**
- **4 egg yolks**
- **½ cup freshly squeezed and strained lemon juice (about 3 to 4 lemons)**
- **2 tablespoons grated lemon peel**
- **2 tablespoons butter**

MERINGUE

- **1 tablespoon cornstarch**
- **⅓ cup water**
- **½ teaspoon vanilla**
- **½ cup sugar, divided**
- **4 egg whites**
- **¼ teaspoon cream of tartar**
  Pie Pastry for One-Crust Pie, baked (page 116)

1 Preheat oven to 350°F. For filling, combine sugar, water, salt and cornstarch in medium saucepan. Bring to a simmer over medium heat until mixture becomes thick and translucent.

2 Quickly whisk in egg yolks, then add lemon juice, peel and butter. Return to simmer and cook 1 minute.

3 Cover the surface of the filling with plastic wrap to keep hot and prevent a skin from forming. Set aside.

4 For meringue, stir cornstarch into ⅓ cup water in small saucepan until smooth. Stir in 1 tablespoon sugar and vanilla. Cook, stirring frequently, until thick paste forms. Remove from heat and cool.

5 Attach wire whip to stand mixer. Beat egg whites in mixer bowl until foamy.

6 In separate bowl, combine remaining sugar and cream of tartar; add to egg whites in two batches, beating until soft peaks form. Add cornstarch mixture 1 tablespoon at a time, beating until stiff peaks form.

7 Pour hot pie filling into crust. Spread meringue over filling, covering completely. Bake 12 to 15 minutes or until the peaks of meringue are golden brown. Let cool before serving.

BOSTON CREAM PIE

MAKES 8 SERVINGS

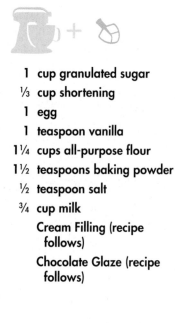

1 **cup granulated sugar**

⅓ **cup shortening**

1 **egg**

1 **teaspoon vanilla**

1¼ **cups all-purpose flour**

1½ **teaspoons baking powder**

½ **teaspoon salt**

¾ **cup milk**

Cream Filling (recipe follows)

Chocolate Glaze (recipe follows)

MELTING CHOCOLATE

Chocolate burns and sticks to the pan easily, so when melting chocolate over an open flame, it is important to keep the heat low and stir constantly.

1 Preheat oven to 350°F. Grease and flour 9-inch round cake pan. Beat granulated sugar and shortening in bowl of electric stand mixer until light and fluffy. Blend in egg and vanilla. Combine flour, baking powder and salt in small bowl. Add flour mixture to sugar mixture alternately with milk, beating after each addition. Pour into prepared pan.

2 Bake 35 minutes or until toothpick inserted in center comes out clean. Cool in pan 10 minutes. Loosen edge of cake and remove to rack to cool completely.

3 Meanwhile, prepare Cream Filling and Chocolate Glaze. When cake is cool, split in half horizontally. To assemble, spoon Cream Filling over bottom half of cake; cover with top half. Spread top with Chocolate Glaze; let stand until glaze is set. Refrigerate leftovers.

Cream Filling: Combine ⅓ cup granulated sugar, 2 tablespoons cornstarch and ¼ teaspoon salt in 2-quart saucepan. Gradually stir in 1½ cups milk. Cook over medium heat, stirring constantly, until mixture thickens and comes to a boil. Boil 1 minute, stirring constantly. Gradually stir small amount of hot mixture into 2 slightly beaten egg yolks; mix thoroughly. Return to hot mixture in pan. Bring to a boil; boil 1 minute, stirring constantly. Do not overcook. Remove from heat; stir in 2 teaspoons vanilla. Cool to room temperature. Chill.

Chocolate Glaze: Combine 2 (1-ounce) squares unsweetened chocolate and 3 tablespoons butter in medium saucepan; stir over low heat until melted. Remove from heat; stir in 1 cup sifted powdered sugar and 1 teaspoon vanilla. Stir in 3 to 5 teaspoons water, 1 teaspoon at a time, until glaze is of desired consistency. Cool slightly.

BANANA CREAM PIE

MAKES 8 SERVINGS

Pie Pastry for One-Crust Pie (page 116)
- 3 **bananas, divided**
- 1 **teaspoon lemon juice**
- ½ **cup sugar**
- 6 **tablespoons cornstarch**
- ¼ **teaspoon salt**
- 3 **cups milk**
- 2 **egg yolks**
- 2 **tablespoons butter**
- 1½ **teaspoons vanilla**
  Sweetened whipped cream
  Ground cinnamon

1 Preheat oven to 400°F. Prick holes in bottom of crust with fork. Bake 10 minutes or until lightly browned. Transfer to wire rack; cool. Slice 2 bananas; toss with lemon juice. Layer on bottom of crust.

2 Combine sugar, cornstarch and salt in medium saucepan. Combine milk and egg yolks in medium bowl; slowly stir into sugar mixture. Cook over medium heat, stirring constantly until mixture is thickened. Boil 1 minute, stirring constantly. Remove from heat; stir in vanilla and pour into crust. Immediately cover with waxed paper. Refrigerate 2 hours or until ready to serve.

3 Remove waxed paper and slice remaining banana. Arrange slices around edge of pie. Garnish with whipped cream and cinnamon.

MAKING SWEETENED WHIPPED CREAM

Combine ½ cup cold whipping cream, 1 tablespoon powdered sugar and ¼ teaspoon vanilla in mixer bowl. Whip at high speed until soft peaks form. For best results, make sure your mixer bowl, whip attachment and cream are very cold.

LATTICE-TOPPED CHERRY PIE

MAKES 8 SERVINGS

6 cups pitted sweet Bing cherries

¾ cup sugar

3 tablespoons cornstarch

2 tablespoons lemon juice

1 unbaked Pie Pastry for Two-Crust Pie (page 116)
Half-and-half
Granulated sugar

TIP

For a classic sour cherry pie, use fresh pitted sour cherries, omit lemon juice, and increase sugar to 1½ cups.

If cherries aren't in season, either sweet or sour frozen cherries will work just as well. Simply thaw and drain before combining with sugar in step 2.

1 Preheat oven to 400°F.

2 Combine cherries, sugar, cornstarch and lemon juice in bowl, mixing to coat cherries. Let stand 15 minutes or until a syrup forms.

3 Meanwhile, prepare Pie Pastry. Roll out half of pastry and fit into 9-inch pie pan. Roll out second sheet of pastry into rectangle. Cut into 12 to 14 strips about ½-inch wide.

4 Pour cherry filling into bottom crust. Lay 6 to 7 pastry strips horizontally over crust. Weave in remaining strips. Tuck strips under bottom crust and press to seal.

5 Brush crust with half-and-half; sprinkle with additional sugar.

6 Cover with foil. Bake 30 minutes. Remove foil and continue baking 20 to 25 minutes or until crust is golden brown and filling is thick and bubbly. Cool on wire rack.

VANILLA CREAM PIE

MAKES 8 SERVINGS

- 1 **cup sugar, divided**
- 6 **tablespoons all-purpose flour**
- ¼ **teaspoon plus ⅛ teaspoon salt, divided**
- 2½ **cups milk**
- 3 **eggs, separated**
- 1 **tablespoon butter**
- 1 **teaspoon vanilla**
  Pie Pastry for One-Crust Pie, baked (page 116)
- ¼ **teaspoon cream of tartar**

FLAKED COCONUT

Adding coconut is an easy and delicious way to spice up your vanilla cream pie for a special occasion. Consider adding toasted coconut as a garnish for extra flavor.

1 Preheat oven to 325°F. Combine ½ cup sugar, flour, and ¼ teaspoon salt in heavy saucepan. Add milk and cook over medium heat until thickened, stirring constantly. Reduce heat to low. Cook, covered, about 10 minutes longer, stirring occasionally. Set aside.

2 Place egg yolks in bowl of electric stand mixer. Turn to high and whip about 1 minute. Slowly stir small amount of milk mixture into yolks. Add yolk mixture to saucepan. Cook over medium heat 3 to 4 minutes, stirring constantly. Remove from heat. Stir in butter and vanilla; cool. Pour into baked crust.

3 Place cream of tartar, remaining ⅛ teaspoon salt and egg whites in clean mixer bowl. Gradually turn to high and whip about 1 minute or until soft peaks form. Turn speed to medium-low. Gradually add remaining sugar and whip about 1 minute or until stiff peaks form.

4 Lightly pile meringue on pie and spread to edge. Bake 15 minutes or until lightly browned.

Chocolate Cream Pie: Melt 2 squares (1 ounce each) unsweetened chocolate and add to filling along with butter and vanilla. Proceed as directed above.

Coconut Cream Pie: Add ½ cup sweetened flaked coconut to filling before pouring into baked crust. Before baking, sprinkle ¼ cup flaked coconut on meringue. Proceed as directed above.

ONION, CHEESE AND TOMATO TART

MAKES 6 TO 8 SERVINGS

Parmesan-Pepper Dough (recipe follows)
1 tablespoon butter
1 medium onion, thinly sliced
1 cup (4 ounces) shredded Swiss cheese
2 to 3 ripe tomatoes, sliced
Black pepper
2 tablespoons chopped fresh chives

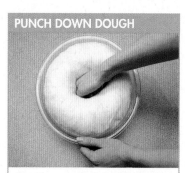

PUNCH DOWN DOUGH

To effectively punch down yeast dough, push your fist into the center of the dough. Continue using your fist to push the sides of the dough into the center until you feel that the dough is deflated and all the air is gone.

1 Prepare Parmesan-Pepper Dough.

2 Melt butter in large skillet over medium heat. Add onion; cook and stir 20 minutes or until tender.

3 Spread onion over dough. Sprinkle with cheese. Let rise in warm place 20 to 30 minutes or until edges are puffy.

4 Preheat oven to 400°F. Top dough with tomatoes. Sprinkle with pepper. Bake 25 minutes or until edges are deep golden and cheese is melted. Let cool 10 minutes. Transfer to serving platter. Sprinkle with chives. Cut into wedges before serving.

PARMESAN-PEPPER DOUGH

1 package (¼ ounce) active dry yeast
1 tablespoon sugar
⅔ cup warm water (105° to 115°F)
2 cups all-purpose flour, divided
¼ cup grated Parmesan cheese
1 teaspoon salt
½ teaspoon black pepper
1 tablespoon olive oil

1 Sprinkle yeast and sugar over warm water in small bowl; stir until yeast is dissolved. Let stand 5 minutes or until mixture is bubbly.

2 Combine 1¾ cups flour, cheese, salt and pepper in bowl of electric stand mixer; mix at low speed 1 minute or until combined. Pour yeast mixture and oil over flour mixture; mix at medium-low until mixture clings together.

3 Attach dough hook to mixer. Knead 2 to 3 minutes at low speed or until dough is smooth and elastic, adding remaining ¼ cup flour if necessary. Shape dough into ball. Place in large greased bowl; turn to grease top. Cover; let rise in warm place 1 hour or until doubled in bulk.

4 Punch down dough. Knead on lightly floured surface 1 minute or until smooth. Flatten into disc. Roll dough into 11-inch circle. Press into bottom and up side of buttered 9- or 10-inch tart pan with removable bottom.

STRAWBERRY CREAM PIE

MAKES 8 SERVINGS

- 1 cup plus 1½ teaspoons all-purpose flour, divided
- ¼ cup plus 1 teaspoon sugar, divided
- ¼ teaspoon salt
- ¼ cup (½ stick) cold butter, cut into pieces
- 3 tablespoons ice water, divided
- ¾ teaspoon white or cider vinegar
- 8 ounces Neufchâtel cheese
- ¼ cup vanilla yogurt
- 2 egg whites
- ½ teaspoon vanilla
- 1½ cups fresh strawberries, cut in half
- ¼ cup strawberry jelly

1 Preheat oven to 450°F. Combine 1 cup flour, 1 teaspoon sugar and salt in medium bowl. Cut in butter with pastry blender or two knives until coarse crumbs form. Add 2 tablespoons ice water and vinegar; stir until moist but slightly firm dough forms. If necessary, add remaining 1 tablespoon ice water. Form dough into ball.

2 Roll out dough into 12-inch circle on lightly floured surface. Place in 9-inch glass pie dish. Bake 10 to 12 minutes or until lightly browned. Cool on wire rack. *Reduce oven temperature to 325°F.*

3 Beat Neufchâtel, remaining ¼ cup sugar and 1½ teaspoons flour in bowl of electric stand mixer at medium speed until creamy. Beat in yogurt, egg whites and vanilla; mix well. Pour into crust. Bake 25 minutes or until set. Cool completely on wire rack.

4 Place strawberries on top of filling. For glaze, melt jelly over low heat in small saucepan; brush over strawberries. Refrigerate 3 hours or overnight. Cut into 8 wedges.

GLAZING STRAWBERRIES

When glazing strawberries or any other type of berry, use a pastry brush and gentle strokes. You want to create a uniform layer of glaze without moving the fruit. The glaze thickens as it cools and becomes difficult to work with, so always apply it while still warm and spreadable.

RUSTIC PLUM TART

MAKES 8 SERVINGS

1 unbaked Pie Pastry for
  One-Crust Pie (page 116)
¼ cup (½ stick) plus
  1 tablespoon butter,
  divided
3 cups plum wedges (about
  6 medium, see Tip)
¼ cup granulated sugar
½ cup all-purpose flour
½ cup old-fashioned or quick
  oats
¼ cup packed brown sugar
½ teaspoon ground cinnamon
¼ teaspoon salt
1 egg
1 teaspoon water
1 tablespoon chopped
  crystallized ginger*

*Crystallized ginger can be found
in the baking aisle or Asian food
section of the supermarket.*

TIP

*For this recipe, use dark
reddish-purple plums and
cut the fruit into 8 wedges.*

1 Preheat oven to 425°F. Line baking sheet with parchment paper. Prepare Pie Pastry; do not place in pie plate.

2 Melt 1 tablespoon butter in large skillet over high heat. Add plums; cook and stir 3 minutes or until plums are softened. Stir in granulated sugar; cook 1 minute or until juices have thickened. Remove from heat; set aside.

3 Combine flour, oats, brown sugar, cinnamon and salt in medium bowl. Cut in remaining ¼ cup butter with pastry blender or two knives until mixture resembles coarse crumbs.

4 Beat egg and water in small bowl. Roll out pie pastry into 10-inch circle on prepared baking sheet. Brush lightly with egg mixture. Sprinkle with ¼ cup oat mixture, leaving 2-inch border around edge of crust. Spoon plums over oat mixture, leaving juices in skillet. Sprinkle with ginger. Fold crust edge up around plums, overlapping as necessary. Sprinkle with remaining oat mixture. Brush edge of crust with egg mixture.

5 Bake 25 minutes or until golden brown. Cool slightly before serving.

CUTTING IN BUTTER

Cutting in butter is the process by which dry ingredients and fat (butter or shortening) are combined. It is a crucial step in many baking recipes.

SWEET POTATO PECAN PIE

MAKES 8 SERVINGS

1 unbaked Pie Pastry for
   One-Crust Pie (page 116)
1½ cups pecan halves
½ cup light corn syrup
1 egg white
2 cups puréed cooked sweet
   potatoes
⅓ cup packed brown sugar
1 teaspoon vanilla
½ teaspoon ground cinnamon
¼ teaspoon salt
   Pinch each ground nutmeg
   and ground cloves
2 eggs, beaten

1 Preheat oven to 400°F. Prick holes in bottom of pie crust with fork. Bake 10 minutes or until very lightly browned and dry; remove from oven. *Reduce oven temperature to 350°F.*

2 Combine pecans, corn syrup and egg white in small bowl; mix well. Set aside.

3 Combine sweet potatoes, brown sugar, vanilla, cinnamon, salt, nutmeg and cloves in bowl of electric stand mixer; mix until well blended. Stir in eggs.

4 Spread sweet potato mixture into prepared pie crust. Spoon pecan mixture evenly over top. Bake 45 to 50 minutes or until filling is puffed and topping is golden. Cool completely on wire rack.

APPLE PIE

MAKES 8 SERVINGS.

1 Preheat oven to 400°F. Combine 1 cup sugar, flour, cinnamon, nutmeg and salt in large bowl. Stir in apples.

2 Fill bottom crust with apple mixture; dot with butter. Cover with top pastry crust. Seal and crimp edge; cut slits to vent. Sprinkle with sugar, if desired.

3 Bake 50 minutes or until crust is golden brown.

1 **cup sugar, plus additional for topping**

2 **tablespoons all-purpose flour**

1 **teaspoon cinnamon**

⅛ **teaspoon nutmeg**

⅛ **teaspoon salt**

6 **to 8 medium tart cooking apples, peeled, cored, and thinly sliced**

1 **unbaked Pie Pastry for Two-Crust Pie (page 116)**

2 **tablespoons butter**

COATING APPLES

Coat the apples completely with the spice mixture before placing them in the pie crust. An even distribution of ingredients will result in a better tasting pie.

QUICK BREADS

Weekday mornings quickly become special when sweet breads, scones and biscuits replace cereal and toast

DATE NUT BREAD

MAKES 12 SERVINGS

2 cups all-purpose flour
½ cup packed light brown sugar
1 tablespoon baking powder
½ teaspoon salt
¼ cup (½ stick) cold butter, cut into pieces
1 cup toasted chopped walnuts
1 cup chopped dates
1¼ cups milk
1 egg
½ teaspoon grated lemon peel

1 Preheat oven to 375°F. Spray 9×5-inch loaf pan with nonstick cooking spray.

2 Combine flour, brown sugar, baking powder and salt in bowl of electric stand mixer. With mixer on low, cut in butter until mixture resembles fine crumbs. Add walnuts and dates; stir until coated.

3 Beat milk, egg and lemon peel in medium bowl. Stir into flour mixture just until moistened. Spread in prepared pan.

4 Bake 45 to 50 minutes or until toothpick inserted into center comes out clean. Cool in pan on wire rack 10 minutes. Remove from pan; cool completely on wire rack.

DILL SOUR CREAM SCONES

MAKES 12 SCONES

2 cups all-purpose flour

2 teaspoons baking powder

½ teaspoon baking soda

½ teaspoon salt

¼ cup (½ stick) cold butter, cut into pieces

2 eggs

½ cup sour cream

1 tablespoon chopped fresh dill or 1 teaspoon dried dill weed

1 Preheat oven to 425°F.

2 Combine flour, baking powder, baking soda and salt in bowl of electric stand mixer. With mixer on low, cut in butter until mixture resembles coarse crumbs. Beat eggs, sour cream and dill in medium bowl well blended. Stir into flour mixture until mixture forms soft dough that pulls away from side of bowl.

3 Turn out dough onto floured surface. Knead 10 times. Roll dough into 9×6-inch rectangle with lightly floured rolling pin. Cut dough into 6 (3-inch) squares. Cut each square diagonally in half, making 12 triangles. Place triangles 2 inches apart on ungreased baking sheets.

4 Bake 10 to 12 minutes or until golden brown and toothpick inserted into centers comes out clean. Cool on wire rack 10 minutes. Serve warm or cool completely.

FOLDING THE DOUGH

To knead dough, fold dough in half toward you and press dough away from you with heels of hands.

KNEADING THE DOUGH

Give dough a quarter turn and continue folding, pushing and turning.

BASIC CREAM SCONES

MAKES 8 SCONES

2¼ **cups all-purpose flour**
¼ **cup granulated sugar**
1 **tablespoon baking powder**
½ **teaspoon salt**
6 **tablespoons cold unsalted butter, cut into pieces**
⅔ **cup whipping cream**
2 **eggs, beaten**
   Coarse white decorating sugar

SUGAR GLAZE

When making a glaze with powdered sugar, always be sure to sift the powdered sugar beforehand. This will ensure that your glaze has a smooth, lump-free consistency.

1 Preheat oven to 425°F. Combine flour, granulated sugar, baking powder and salt in bowl of electric stand mixer. With mixer on low, cut in butter until mixture resembles coarse crumbs.

2 Combine cream and eggs in small bowl; reserve 1 tablespoon egg mixture. Pour remaining egg mixture over flour mixture. Stir just until moistened.

3 Turn out dough onto lightly floured surface. Shape into ball; pat into 8-inch disc. Cut into 8 wedges; place 2 inches apart on ungreased baking sheet. Brush reserved egg mixture over tops; sprinkle with coarse sugar.

4 Bake 12 to 14 minutes or until golden. Remove to wire rack to cool completely.

Chocolate Lavender Scones: Add 1 teaspoon dried lavender to dry ingredients. Stir ½ cup coarsely chopped semisweet chocolate into dough before shaping.

Ginger Peach Scones: Stir ⅓ cup chopped dried peaches and 1 tablespoon finely chopped crystallized ginger into dough before shaping.

Lemon Poppy Seed Scones: Stir grated peel of 1 lemon (about 3½ teaspoons) and 1 tablespoon poppy seeds into dough before shaping. Omit coarse sugar topping. Combine 1 cup powdered sugar and 2 tablespoons lemon juice (add up to 1½ teaspoons more lemon juice, if necessary, for desired consistency). Drizzle over slightly cooled scones.

Maple Pecan Scones: Stir ½ cup coarsely chopped pecans into dough before shaping. Omit coarse sugar topping. Combine ¾ cup powdered sugar and 2 tablespoons maple syrup. Drizzle over slightly cooled scones.

Mini Scones: Divide dough into 2 balls before shaping into rounds and cutting into wedges. Makes 16 scones.

Round Scones: Cut dough into rounds using lightly floured cookie or biscuit cutter.

LEMON-CARDAMOM SCONES WITH LEMON DRIZZLE

MAKES 8 SERVINGS

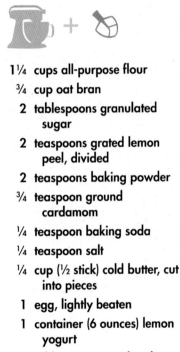

1¼ cups all-purpose flour

¾ cup oat bran

2 tablespoons granulated sugar

2 teaspoons grated lemon peel, divided

2 teaspoons baking powder

¾ teaspoon ground cardamom

¼ teaspoon baking soda

¼ teaspoon salt

¼ cup (½ stick) cold butter, cut into pieces

1 egg, lightly beaten

1 container (6 ounces) lemon yogurt

3 tablespoons powdered sugar

2 teaspoons lemon juice

1 Preheat oven to 400°F. Lightly coat baking sheet with nonstick cooking spray.

2 Combine flour, oat bran, granulated sugar, 1½ teaspoons lemon peel, baking powder, cardamom, baking soda and salt in bowl of electric stand mixer. With mixer on low, cut in butter until mixture resembles coarse crumbs.

3 Stir together egg and yogurt in small bowl until blended. Pour egg mixture into flour mixture; stir just until moistened. Turn out dough onto lightly floured surface. Gently knead dough 10 to 12 times. Pat dough into 7½-inch circle. Cut into 8 wedges. Place wedges 2 inches apart on prepared baking sheet.

4 Bake 11 to 13 minutes or until scones are golden brown. Remove to wire rack; cool 10 minutes. Stir together powdered sugar, lemon juice and remaining ½ teaspoon lemon peel until smooth; drizzle over scones.

Lemon-Ginger Scones: Substitute ground ginger for ground cardamom.

LEMON PEEL

Freshly grated lemon peel provides a flavor that dried lemon peel can't match. One medium lemon equals approximately 1 tablespoon of grated lemon peel. When grating lemon peel, avoid the bitter white portion known as the pith.

CRANBERRY-ORANGE SCONES

MAKES 12 SCONES

½ **cup dried cranberries**

1 **cup hot water**

3¾ **cups Better Baking Mix (recipe follows)**

¼ **cup sugar**

¼ **cup (½ stick) cold butter, cut into pieces**

1¼ **cups cold fat-free (skim) milk or low-fat buttermilk**

1 **tablespoon grated orange peel**

Ground cinnamon (optional)

DRIED CRANBERRIES

Soaking the dried cranberries in water before adding them to the dough softens and plumps them up so they will have a better consistency in the finished scones.

1 Preheat oven to 400°F. Lightly spray baking sheet with nonstick cooking spray. Soak cranberries in hot water about 10 minutes or until softened; drain.

2 Meanwhile, combine 3¾ cups Better Baking Mix and sugar in bowl of electric stand mixer. With mixer on low, cut in butter until mixture resembles coarse crumbs. Add milk; stir together just until mixed. Gently fold in drained cranberries and orange peel.

3 Scoop 12 pieces of dough 1-inch apart onto baking sheet, using ¼-cup measure or 2-inch ice cream scoop. (Dip the cup or scoop in water between scoops to help the batter release easier.) Sprinkle lightly with cinnamon.

4 Bake 10 to 12 minutes, rotating baking sheet once during baking, or until scones are golden brown on tops and toothpick inserted into centers comes out clean. Serve immediately or cool on wire rack.

BETTER BAKING MIX

2¼ **cups all-purpose flour**

2¼ **cups whole wheat flour**

2¼ **cups oat flour**

1¼ **cups nonfat dry milk powder**

3 **tablespoons baking powder**

1½ **teaspoons salt**

1 **teaspoon baking soda**

Combine all ingredients in large resealable food storage bag. Stir with wire whisk. Seal bag; shake to thoroughly mix. Store in refrigerator. Makes about 8 cups.

CHOCOLATE CHIP ZUCCHINI BREAD

MAKES 2 LOAVES

- 2 **small zucchini**
- 3 **eggs**
- 2 **cups sugar**
- 1 **cup (2 sticks) melted butter**
- 1 **teaspoon vanilla**
- ⅓ **cup unsweetened cocoa powder**
- 1 **small seedless orange**
- 2 **cups all-purpose flour**
- 1 **teaspoon baking soda**
- 1 **teaspoon salt**
- 1 **teaspoon ground cinnamon**
- ¾ **cup semisweet chocolate chips**

1 Preheat oven to 350°F. Lightly grease 2 (9×5-inch) loaf pans. Fit food processor with steel blade. Grate zucchini; squeeze dry and set aside.

2 Combine eggs, sugar, butter, grated zucchini, vanilla and cocoa powder in bowl of electric stand mixer. Mix on low until well blended.

3 Grind the orange (including rind) in food processer. Stir into zucchini mixture.

4 Stir in flour, baking soda, salt and cinnamon. Fold in chocolate chips.

5 Pour batter into loaf pans. Bake 1 hour or until toothpick inserted into centers comes out clean.

BAKING POWDER BISCUITS
MAKES 12 BISCUITS

1 Preheat oven to 450°F. Combine flour, baking powder and salt in bowl of electric stand mixer. With mixer on low, cut in shortening until mixture resembles coarse crumbs.

2 Continuing on low, add milk and mix until dough starts to cling to beater. (Do not overbeat.) Turn out dough onto lightly floured surface and knead about 20 seconds, or until smooth. Pat or roll to ½-inch thickness. Cut with floured 2-inch biscuit cutter.

3 Place on greased baking sheets and brush with melted butter. Bake 12 to 15 minutes. Serve immediately.

2 **cups all-purpose flour**
4 **teaspoons baking powder**
½ **teaspoon salt**
⅓ **cup cold shortening**
⅔ **cup milk**
   Melted butter

HAM & SWISS CHEESE BISCUITS

MAKES ABOUT 18 BISCUITS

2 cups all-purpose flour

2 teaspoons baking powder

½ teaspoon baking soda

½ cup (1 stick) cold butter, cut into pieces

½ cup (2 ounces) shredded Swiss cheese

2 ounces ham, minced

⅔ cup buttermilk

1 Preheat oven to 450°F. Grease baking sheet.

2 Sift flour, baking powder and baking soda into bowl of electric stand mixer. With mixer on low, cut in butter until mixture resembles coarse crumbs. Stir in cheese, ham and enough buttermilk to make soft dough.

3 Turn out dough onto lightly floured surface; knead lightly. Roll out dough ½ inch thick. Cut out biscuits with 2-inch round cutter. Place on prepared baking sheet.

4 Bake about 10 minutes or until browned.

CORNMEAL SCONES
MAKES 16 SERVINGS

1 Preheat oven to 375°F. Lightly spray baking sheet with nonstick cooking spray. Place currants in small bowl. Add water; let stand 10 minutes. Drain and discard water.

2 Combine flour, cornmeal, ½ cup sugar, baking powder, baking soda and salt in bowl of electric stand mixer. With mixer on low, cut butter into flour mixture until mixture resembles coarse crumbs. Stir in currants.

3 Combine yogurt, milk and whole egg in small bowl. Add to flour mixture, stirring just until dry ingredients are moistened. Turn out dough onto lightly floured surface; knead 5 or 6 times. Shape dough into 8-inch round. Place on prepared baking sheet. Brush with egg white; sprinkle with remaining 1 teaspoon sugar. Cut into 8 wedges. Bake 20 minutes or until lightly browned. Place on wire rack to cool. Cut each wedge in half.

½ cup dried currants
1 cup warm water
1⅓ cups all-purpose flour
⅔ cup cornmeal
½ cup plus 1 teaspoon sugar, divided
1½ teaspoons baking powder
½ teaspoon baking soda
¼ teaspoon salt
¼ cup (½ stick) cold butter, cut into 4 pieces
¼ cup plain yogurt
3 tablespoons milk
1 egg, lightly beaten
1 egg white, lightly beaten

HONEY SCONES WITH CHERRY COMPOTE

MAKES 8 SCONES

- 2 **cups all-purpose flour**
- ½ **cup old-fashioned oats**
- 2 **tablespoons packed brown sugar**
- 1 **tablespoon granulated sugar**
- 1 **tablespoon baking powder**
- ½ **teaspoon salt**
- 6 **tablespoons butter, melted and cooled**
- ¼ **cup heavy cream**
- ¼ **cup milk**
- 1 **egg**
- 3 **tablespoons honey**
  Cherry Compote (recipe follows)

1 Preheat oven to 425°F. Line baking sheet with parchment paper.

2 Place flour, oats, sugars, baking powder and salt in bowl of electric stand mixer; stir until blended. Whisk together butter, cream, milk, egg and honey in separate bowl. With mixer on low, add butter mixture to flour mixture. Stir just until dough forms.

3 Turn out dough onto lightly floured surface. Pat dough into 8-inch round, about ¾-inch thick. Cut into 8 wedges. Place 1 to 2 inches apart on prepared baking sheet.

4 Bake 12 to 15 minutes until scones are golden brown. Cool on wire racks 15 minutes. Serve with butter and Cherry Compote.

CHERRY COMPOTE

- 1 **pound pitted fresh Bing cherries***
- ¼ **cup sugar**
- ¼ **cup water**
- 2 **tablespoons freshly squeezed lemon juice**

If cherries are not in season, substitute thawed frozen sweet or sour cherries.

1 Combine all ingredients in heavy saucepan. Bring to a boil over medium heat. Boil 2 minutes. Remove cherries with slotted spoon; set aside.

2 Reduce heat to medium-low; simmer liquid 2 to 4 minutes or until thickened. Remove from heat. Stir in cherries. Cool 1 hour before serving.

CHERRY SCONES

MAKES 8 SCONES

1½ **cups all-purpose flour**

1 **cup whole wheat flour**

3 **tablespoons granulated sugar**

2 **teaspoons baking powder**

¼ **teaspoon salt**

½ **cup cold butter-flavored shortening**

½ **cup honey beer**

⅓ **cup milk**

1 **egg, beaten**

¾ **cup dried cherries**

1 **teaspoon raw sugar**

1 Preheat oven to 425°F. Combine flours, granulated sugar, baking powder and salt in bowl of electric stand mixer. With mixer on low, cut in shortening until mixture resembles coarse crumbs. Combine beer, milk and egg in medium bowl; stir into flour mixture. Stir in cherries. Turn out dough onto floured surface; knead gently 4 times.

2 Shape dough into ball and place on ungreased baking sheet. Pat into 8-inch circle. Score dough into 8 wedges (do not separate). Sprinkle with raw sugar. Bake 18 to 22 minutes or until golden brown. Cut into wedges.

PARMESAN PEPPERCORN BISCUITS

MAKES 12 BISCUITS

1 Preheat oven to 425°F. Line baking sheet with parchment paper.

2 Combine flour, Parmesan, baking powder, pepper and salt in bowl of electric stand mixer. With mixer on low, cut in butter until mixture resembles coarse crumbs. Stir in buttermilk; mix just until moistened.

3 Drop ¼-cup mounds of dough onto prepared baking sheet. Bake 12 to 15 minutes or until tops of biscuits are golden brown. Cool on wire rack 3 to 5 minutes before serving.

- **2** cups all-purpose flour
- **⅓** cup finely grated Parmesan cheese
- **1** tablespoon baking powder
- **1** teaspoon freshly ground black pepper
- **½** teaspoon salt
- **6** tablespoons (¾ stick) cold butter, cut into pieces
- **1** cup buttermilk

SWEET CHERRY BISCUITS

MAKES 6 BISCUITS

- 2 cups flour
- 2 tablespoons sugar
- 4 teaspoons baking powder
- ½ teaspoon salt
- ½ teaspoon crushed dried rosemary
- ½ cup (1 stick) cold unsalted butter, cut into pieces
- ¾ cup milk
- ½ cup dried sweetened cherries, chopped

1 Preheat oven to 425°F. Combine flour, sugar, baking powder, salt and rosemary in bowl of electric stand mixer. With mixer on low, cut in butter until mixture resembles coarse crumbs. Stir in milk to form a sticky batter. Stir in cherries.

2 Remove dough to lightly floured work surface. Pat dough to 1-inch thickness. Cut into circles using a 3-inch biscuit cutter. Place biscuits 1 inch apart on ungreased baking sheet. Bake on center rack of oven until golden brown, about 15 minutes. Remove from oven. Cool on wire rack for 5 minutes before serving.

CHEDDAR & ONION DROP BISCUITS

MAKES 12 BISCUITS

1 Preheat oven to 400°F.

2 Place Better Baking Mix in bowl of electric stand mixer. With mixer on low, cut in oil until mixture resembles coarse crumbs. Add milk; mix on low speed just until moistened. (Do not overmix.) Remove bowl from mixer. Gently fold in cheese and onions with spatula.

3 Using ¼-cup measure, scoop 12 pieces of dough onto baking sheet, placing 1 inch apart. (Dip the cup in water between scoops to help the batter release more easily.)

4 Bake 10 to 12 minutes or until biscuits are golden brown, rotating pan once during baking. Remove to wire rack; serve warm.

3¾ **cups Better Baking Mix (page 148)**

¼ **cup canola oil**

1¼ **cups cold fat-free (skim) milk, low-fat buttermilk or soymilk**

¼ **cup (1 ounce) shredded reduced-fat Cheddar cheese or soy cheese**

¼ **cup sliced green onions**

GREEN ONIONS

Green onions, sometimes called scallions, add a mild onion flavor to savory dishes. Both the green and white parts of the green onion can be used in cooking and baking.

CRANBERRY & WHITE CHOCOLATE SCONES

MAKES 8 SCONES

1 cup all-purpose flour
1 cup whole wheat flour
¼ cup plus 1 tablespoon sugar, divided
2 teaspoons baking powder
½ teaspoon salt
½ teaspoon ground nutmeg
6 tablespoons cold butter, cut into pieces
1 cup dried cranberries
1 cup white chocolate chips
2 eggs
⅓ cup plus 1 tablespoon whipping cream, divided
Grated peel of 1 orange (3 to 4 teaspoons)

1 Preheat oven to 425°F. Line baking sheet with parchment paper. Combine all-purpose flour, whole wheat flour, ¼ cup sugar, baking powder, salt and nutmeg in bowl of electric stand mixer. With mixer on low, cut in butter until mixture resembles coarse crumbs. Stir in cranberries and white chips.

2 Beat eggs in small bowl; whisk in ⅓ cup cream and orange peel. Add to flour mixture; mix on low until dough forms. Knead dough 8 to 10 times on lightly floured surface.

3 Press into 9-inch circle on prepared baking sheet. Score dough into 8 wedges with sharp knife. Brush with remaining 1 tablespoon cream; sprinkle with remaining 1 tablespoon sugar.

4 Bake 20 to 23 minutes or until edges are lightly browned and toothpick inserted into center comes out clean. Remove to cutting board; cut into wedges along score lines. Cool on wire rack.

MUSTARD BEER BISCUITS

MAKES ABOUT 12 BISCUITS

1 Preheat oven to 425°F. Grease large baking sheet.

2 Combine flour, baking powder and salt in bowl of electric stand mixer. With mixer on low, cut in shortening and butter until mixture resembles coarse crumbs. Combine beer and 1 tablespoon mustard in small bowl; stir into flour mixture and mix just until blended. Turn onto floured surface; knead gently 8 times.

3 Pat dough to ½-inch thickness. Cut out biscuits with 2-inch round biscuit cutter. Place 1 inch apart on prepared baking sheet. Combine remaining 1 teaspoon mustard with milk in small bowl and brush over tops. Bake 13 to 15 minutes or until lightly browned.

- **2 cups all-purpose flour**
- **2 teaspoons baking powder**
- **¾ teaspoon salt**
- **¼ cup cold shortening**
- **¼ cup (½ stick) cold butter, cut into pieces**
- **½ cup beer**
- **1 tablespoon plus 1 teaspoon yellow mustard, divided**
- **1 tablespoon milk**

YEAST BREADS

Any rainy day can be brightened by
the aroma of freshly baked bread

WHOLE GRAIN WHEAT BREAD

MAKES 2 LOAVES

- ⅓ cup plus 1 tablespoon brown sugar, divided
- 2 cups warm water (105°F to 115°F)
- 2 packages active dry yeast
- 5 to 6 cups whole wheat flour
- ¾ cup powdered milk
- 2 teaspoons salt
- ⅓ cup vegetable oil

1 Dissolve 1 tablespoon brown sugar in warm water in small bowl. Add yeast and let mixture stand 5 minutes.

2 Place 4 cups flour, powdered milk, ⅓ cup brown sugar and salt in bowl of electric stand mixer. Attach dough hook. Turn to low and mix about 15 seconds. Continuing on low, gradually add yeast mixture and oil; mix 1½ minutes longer. Stop and scrape bowl.

3 Add remaining flour, ½ cup at a time; mix 2 minutes or until dough clings to hook and cleans sides of bowl. Knead 2 minutes on low.

4 Place dough in greased bowl, turning to grease top. Cover; let rise in warm place about 1 hour or until doubled in bulk. Punch dough down and divide in half. Shape each half into loaf. Place in greased 8½×4½-inch loaf pans. Cover; let rise in warm place about 1 hour or until doubled in bulk. Preheat oven to 400°F. Bake 12 minutes. Reduce heat to 350°F; bake 25 minutes or until golden brown. Remove from pans immediately and cool on wire racks.

SCRUMPTIOUS SANDWICH BREAD

MAKES 2 LOAVES

½ **cup low-fat milk**
3 **tablespoons sugar**
3 **tablespoons butter**
2 **teaspoons salt**
2 **packages active dry yeast**
1½ **cups warm water (105°F to 115°F)**
5 **to 6 cups all-purpose flour**

CHECKING FOR DONENESS

You can check yeast breads for doneness by lightly tapping the top of the loaf. If it sounds hollow, then it's ready to be devoured!

1 Place milk, sugar, butter and salt in small saucepan. Heat over low heat until butter melts and sugar dissolves. Cool to lukewarm.

2 Dissolve yeast in warm water in warmed bowl of electric stand mixer. Attach dough hook. Add lukewarm milk mixture and 4½ cups flour. Mix on low 1 minute.

3 Continuing on low, add remaining flour, ½ cup at a time, and mix until dough clings to hook and cleans sides of bowl, about 2 minutes. Knead on low about 2 minutes longer, or until dough is smooth and elastic. Dough will be slightly sticky to the touch.

4 Place dough in greased bowl, turning to grease top. Cover. Let rise in warm place, free from draft, about 1 hour, or until doubled in bulk.

5 Punch dough down and divide in half. Shape each half into a loaf, and place in greased 8½×4½-inch loaf pans. Cover. Let rise in warm place, free from draft, about 1 hour, or until doubled in bulk.

6 Preheat oven to 400°F. Bake loaves 30 minutes or until golden brown. Remove from pans immediately and cool on wire racks.

Sixty-Minute Rolls: Increase yeast to 3 packages and sugar to ¼ cup. Mix and knead dough as directed for Scrumptious Sandwich Bread in steps 2 and 3 above. Place in greased bowl, turning to grease top. Cover. Let rise in warm place, free from draft, about 15 minutes. Turn dough onto lightly floured surface. Shape as desired (see following suggestions). Cover. Let rise in slightly warm oven (90°F) about 15 minutes. Bake at 425°F for 12 minutes, or until golden brown. Remove from pans immediately and cool on wire racks.

Curlicues: Divide dough in half and roll each half to 12×9-inch rectangle. Cut 12 equal strips about 1 inch wide. Roll each strip tightly to form a coil, tucking ends underneath. Place on greased baking sheets about 2 inches apart.

Cloverleafs: Divide dough into 24 equal pieces. Form each piece into a ball and place in greased muffin pan. With scissors, cut each ball in half, then quarters.

FRENCH BREAD
MAKES 2 LOAVES

2 packages active dry yeast
2½ cups warm water (105°F to 115°F)
7 cups all-purpose flour
1 tablespoon butter, melted
1 tablespoon salt
2 tablespoons cornmeal
1 egg white
1 tablespoon cold water

1 Dissolve yeast in warm water in warmed bowl of electric stand mixer. Attach dough hook. Add flour, butter and salt. Mix on low 1 minute or until well blended. Knead on low about 2 minutes longer. Dough will be sticky.

2 Place dough in greased bowl, turning to grease top. Cover. Let rise in warm place, free from draft, about 1 hour, or until doubled in bulk.

3 Punch dough down and divide in half. Roll each half into 12×15-inch rectangle. Roll dough tightly from longest side, tapering ends if desired. Place loaves on greased baking sheets that have been dusted with cornmeal. Cover. Let rise in warm place, free from draft, about 1 hour, or until doubled in bulk.

4 Preheat oven to 450°F. With sharp knife, make 4 diagonal cuts on top of each loaf. Bake 25 minutes. Remove from oven. Beat egg white and water together with a fork. Brush each loaf with egg mixture. Return to oven and bake 5 minutes longer. Remove from baking sheets immediately and cool on wire racks.

IS THE DOUGH DONE RISING?

A good way to check and see if the bread dough has, in fact, doubled in size, is called the touch test. Press the dough on the top with the tips of two fingers. Do this lightly and quickly, and press your fingers about ½ inch into the dough.

If the impression you made stays, then the dough is doubled. If the indent your fingers made quickly disappears, then your dough needs a little bit more time; cover and let rise longer.

SAVORY SUMMERTIME OAT BREAD

MAKES 2 LOAVES

2 carrots

Nonstick cooking spray

½ cup finely chopped onion

2 cups whole wheat flour

4¼ to 4½ cups all-purpose flour, divided

2 cups old-fashioned oats

¼ cup sugar

2 packages (¼ ounce each) rapid-rise active dry yeast*

1½ teaspoons salt

1½ cups water

1¼ cups fat-free (skim) milk

¼ cup butter

3 tablespoons dried parsley flakes

1 tablespoon butter, melted

Rapid-rise and active dry yeast are two types of dry yeast that can be used interchangeably. The advantage of rapid-rise is that the rising time is half that of active dry yeast. However, you do sacrifice some flavor and texture by not allowing the yeast time to fully develop its flavor.

1 Fit processor with steel blade. Grate carrots and measure 1 cup. Spray small nonstick skillet with cooking spray; heat over medium heat. Cook and stir onion 3 minutes or until tender.

2 Attach dough hook to stand mixer. Stir together whole wheat flour, 1 cup all-purpose flour, oats, sugar, yeast and salt in mixer bowl. Heat water, milk and ¼ cup butter in medium saucepan over low heat until mixture reaches 120° to 130°F. Add to flour mixture. Mix at low speed just until dry ingredients are moistened. Stir in carrots, onion, parsley and remaining 3¼ to 3½ cups all-purpose flour. Mix 2 minutes or until dough clings to hook and cleans sides of bowl. Knead on low 2 minutes or until dough is smooth and elastic.

3 Place in large bowl lightly sprayed with cooking spray; turn dough over to coat. Cover and let rise in warm place about 30 minutes or until doubled in bulk. Punch dough down. Cover and let rest 10 minutes.

4 Spray two 8×4-inch loaf pans with cooking spray. Shape dough into 2 loaves; place in pans. Brush with melted butter. Cover; let rise in warm place 30 minutes or until doubled in bulk. Meanwhile, preheat oven to 350°F.

5 Bake 40 to 45 minutes or until bread sounds hollow when tapped. Remove from pans; cool on wire racks.

CINNAMON RAISIN BREAD

MAKES 2 LOAVES

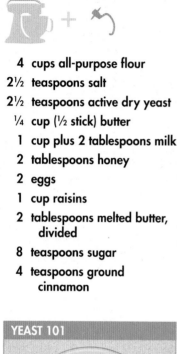

4 **cups all-purpose flour**

2½ **teaspoons salt**

2½ **teaspoons active dry yeast**

¼ **cup (½ stick) butter**

1 **cup plus 2 tablespoons milk**

2 **tablespoons honey**

2 **eggs**

1 **cup raisins**

2 **tablespoons melted butter, divided**

8 **teaspoons sugar**

4 **teaspoons ground cinnamon**

YEAST 101

Yeast is a living organism and can be very sensitive. It needs three things to function properly: food (usually sugar), warmth and moisture.

1 Combine flour, salt and yeast in bowl of electric stand mixer. Melt ¼ cup butter in small saucepan over low heat; stir in milk and honey until mixture is warm but not hot. Add eggs and whisk to combine; remove from heat.

2 Attach dough hook to stand mixture. Add egg mixture and raisins to flour mixture. Mix on low speed until dough clings to hook and cleans sides of bowl. Knead on low 2 minutes.

3 Place dough in lightly oiled bowl, turning to oil top. Cover loosely with plastic wrap. Set in warm place and let rise 1 to 1½ hours or until dough is doubled in bulk.

4 Grease and flour 2 (8×4-inch) loaf pans. Punch down dough and separate into 2 balls. Roll each ball into 8×10×½-inch rectangle. Brush tops with 1 tablespoon melted butter.

5 Combine sugar and cinnamon in small bowl. Reserve 2 teaspoons sugar mixture; sprinkle remaining sugar mixture evenly over dough.

6 Roll up each dough rectangle, starting with short sides, and place in prepared loaf pans. Cover with plastic wrap. Set in warm place and let rise 1 to 1½ hours or until almost doubled in bulk.

7 Preheat oven to 375°F. Bake loaves 35 minutes or until golden brown (internal temperature should register 180°F), rotating pans once. Brush tops with remaining 1 tablespoon melted butter; sprinkle with reserved sugar mixture. Cool in pans 10 minutes. Remove to wire rack; cool completely.

GARLIC PULL-APART BREAD

MAKES 2 LOAVES

6 to 7 cups all-purpose flour,
   divided

3 tablespoons sugar

2 tablespoons garlic salt,
   divided

2 packages active dry yeast

1½ cups water

½ cup milk

½ cup (1 stick) butter, divided

GARLIC BUTTER

*For extra garlic flavor, make
homemade garlic butter to
serve with this bread. Combine
2 minced garlic cloves and 3
tablespoons softened butter.*

1 Place 5 cups flour, sugar, 1 tablespoon garlic salt, and yeast in bowl of electric stand mixer. Attach dough hook to mixer. Turn to low and mix 15 seconds. Combine water, milk and ¼ cup butter in small saucepan. Heat over low heat until liquids are warm (120°F to 130°F).

2 Turn mixer to low and gradually add warm liquids to flour mixture, about 30 seconds. Mix 1 minute longer. Continuing on low, add remaining flour, ½ cup at a time, until dough clings to hook and cleans sides of bowl. Knead on low 2 minutes longer.

3 Place in a greased bowl, turning to grease top. Cover; let rise in warm place, free from draft, until doubled in bulk, about 1 hour.

4 Punch dough down and divide in half. Roll one half into 12×8×¼-inch rectangle. Melt remaining butter and mix with remaining garlic salt. Brush dough with mixture. Cut dough into four equal 8×3-inch strips. Stack strips and cut into four equal 3×2-inch strips. Place pieces on edge in greased 8½×4½-inch loaf pan so strips form one row down length of pan. Repeat with remaining dough. Cover; let rise in warm place, free from draft, until doubled in bulk, about 1 hour. Bake at 400°F for 30 to 35 minutes. Remove from pans immediately and cool on wire racks.

PANETTONE

MAKES 1 LOAF

4 to 4½ cups all-purpose flour, divided

1 teaspoon salt

½ cup raisins

1 teaspoon grated lemon peel

½ cup chopped candied citron

¼ cup sugar

1 package active dry yeast

1 cup warm milk (105°F to 115°F)

½ cup vegetable oil

¼ cup (½ stick) butter, melted

4 egg yolks, beaten

1 egg white

1 tablespoon water

1 Place 3 cups flour, salt, raisins, lemon peel, candied citron and sugar in bowl of electric stand mixer. Attach dough hook to mixer. Turn to low and mix 15 seconds. Dissolve yeast in warm milk; add oil and butter.

2 Turn to low and gradually add warm milk mixture and egg yolks to flour mixture. Mix 1 minute. Continuing on low, add remaining flour, ½ cup at a time, until dough clings to hook* and cleans sides of bowl. Knead on low for 2 minutes longer.

3 Place in greased bowl, turning to grease top. Cover; let rise in warm place, free from draft, until doubled in bulk, about 1 hour.

4 Punch dough down and shape into ball. Place in greased and floured 1½-quart soufflé dish. Let rise, uncovered, in warm place, free from draft, until doubled in bulk, about 1 hour.

5 Preheat oven to 350°F. Cut two slashes with a sharp knife in a cross pattern on top of loaf. Beat egg white and water together with a fork and brush top of loaf with mixture. Bake 55 to 60 minutes. Remove from baking dish immediately and cool on wire rack.

*Dough may not form a ball on hook; however, as long as there is contact between dough and hook, kneading will be accomplished. Do not add more than the maximum amount of flour specified or dry loaf will result.

EGG BAGELS

MAKES 12 BAGELS

½ to ¾ cup warm water
(105° to 115°F), divided

1 package (¼ ounce) active
dry yeast

2 tablespoons plus
1 teaspoon sugar

2½ cups all-purpose flour

1 tablespoon canola oil

1 teaspoon salt

2 large eggs

2 quarts, plus 2 tablespoons
water

FLAVOR IT UP

It's easy to turn your egg bagels into the flavors you find in your favorite deli. After brushing bagels with egg/water mixture, sprinkle with sea salt, poppy seeds, sesame seeds, garlic salt or all of the above!

1 Combine ¼ cup of the warm water, yeast and 1 teaspoon sugar. Stir to dissolve yeast and let stand until bubbly, about 5 minutes.

2 Fit processor with steel blade. Measure flour, oil and salt into work bowl. Cover; process until mixed, about 5 seconds. Add yeast mixture and 1 egg; process until blended, about 10 seconds.

3 Turn on processor and very slowly drizzle just enough remaining warm water through feed tube so dough forms a ball that cleans the sides of the bowl. Process until ball turns around bowl about 25 times. Turn off processor and let dough stand 1 to 2 minutes.

4 Turn on processor and gradually drizzle in enough remaining warm water to make dough soft, smooth and satiny but not sticky. Process until dough turns around bowl about 15 times.

5 Turn dough onto lightly greased surface. Shape into ball and cover with plastic wrap. Let stand about 15 minutes.

6 Divide dough into 12 equal pieces. Shape each piece into a strand about 6 inches long. Bring both ends of each strand together to form a doughnut shape. Moisten ends and pinch together to seal. Place bagels on greased cookie sheet and let stand at room temperature about 15 minutes.

7 Combine remaining 2 quarts water and remaining 2 tablespoons sugar in Dutch oven or stock pot. Bring water to a boil. Gently place 3 or 4 bagels at a time in boiling water. When they rise to the surface, turn them over and cook until puffy, 1½ to 2 minutes longer. Remove bagels from water with a slotted spoon and place on greased cookie sheet.

8 Heat oven to 425°F. Beat remaining egg and 2 tablespoons cold water with a fork. Brush mixture over bagels. Bake until crusts are golden and crisp, 20 to 25 minutes. Remove from cookie sheet. Cool on wire rack.

NEW YORK RYE BREAD

MAKES 2 LOAVES

2 **cups warm water
   (105° to 115°F)**

⅓ **cup packed brown sugar**

1 **tablespoon salt**

2 **tablespoons vegetable oil**

1 **package (¼ ounce) active
   dry yeast**

2 **to 2½ cups bread flour**

1 **tablespoon caraway seeds**

2 **cups rye flour**

1 **cup whole wheat flour**

   Shortening

   Cornmeal

   Bread flour

TIP

*New York rye bread is a
light rye bread, typically
shaped into oblong or round
loaves. Try it for delicious
deli meat sandwiches or
grilled cheese.*

1 Stir together warm water, sugar, salt, oil and yeast in bowl of electric stand mixer until yeast is dissolved.

2 Add 2 cups of bread flour. Attach dough hook to mixer. Mix on low speed about 2 minutes. Gradually stir in caraway seeds, rye and wheat flours, ½ cup at a time, and enough remaining bread flour so dough begins to form a ball and pulls away from the sides of bowl. Continue kneading on low until dough is smooth and elastic.

3 Place dough in greased bowl, turning to grease top. Cover, let rise in warm place 1½ to 2 hours or until doubled in bulk.

4 Grease 1 large or 2 small cookie sheets with shortening. Sprinkle with cornmeal. Punch down dough. Divide in half. Shape each half into a football-shaped loaf, about 10 inches long. Place loaves on cookie sheet(s). Cover; let rise in warm place 45 to 60 minutes or until almost doubled in bulk.

5 Preheat oven to 375°F. Spray or brush loaves with cool water; sprinkle lightly with bread flour. Carefully cut three ¼-inch-deep slashes on top of loaves with sharp serrated knife.

6 Bake 25 to 30 minutes or until loaves sound hollow when tapped. Remove from cookie sheet(s) to wire rack; cool.

THREE-GRAIN BREAD

MAKES 1 LOAF

1 **cup whole wheat flour**
¾ **cup all-purpose flour**
1 **package rapid-rise active**
    dry yeast*
1 **cup milk**
2 **tablespoons honey**
3 **teaspoons olive oil**
1 **teaspoon salt**
½ **cup old-fashioned oats**
¼ **cup whole grain cornmeal**
1 **egg beaten with**
    1 tablespoon water
    (optional)
1 **tablespoon old-fashioned**
    oats for topping (optional)

*Rapid-rise and active dry yeast are two types of dry yeast that can be used interchangeably. The advantage of rapid-rise is that the rising time is half that of active dry yeast. However, you do sacrifice some flavor and texture by not allowing the yeast time to fully develop its flavor.

1 Combine whole wheat flour, all-purpose flour and yeast in bowl of electric stand mixer. Stir milk, honey, olive oil and salt in small saucepan over low heat until warm (110° to 120°F). Attach dough hook to mixer. Stir milk mixture into flour; beat 3 minutes at high speed. Reduce speed to low, and mix in oats and cornmeal. If dough is too wet, add additional flour by teaspoonfuls until it begins to come together.

2 Knead on low until dough clings to hook and cleans sides of bowl. Knead 2 to 3 minutes more or until dough is smooth and elastic. Place dough in large, lightly oiled bowl; turn once to coat. Cover; let rise in warm place about 1 hour or until dough is puffy and does not spring back when touched.

3 Punch dough down and shape into 8-inch long loaf. Place on baking sheet lightly dusted with cornmeal. Cover; let rise in warm place until almost doubled, about 45 minutes. Meanwhile, preheat oven to 375°F.

4 Make shallow slash down center of loaf with sharp knife. Brush lightly with egg mixture and sprinkle with oats, if desired. Bake 30 minutes or until loaf sounds hollow when tapped (internal temperature of 200°F). Remove to wire rack to cool.

PEPPERONI CHEESE BREAD

MAKES 2 LOAVES

1 package (¼ ounce) active
   dry yeast
1 cup warm beer
½ cup warm milk
2¼ cups all-purpose flour,
   divided
1 cup rye flour
1 tablespoon dried basil
1 teaspoon sugar
1 teaspoon salt
1 teaspoon red pepper flakes
1 cup (4 ounces) shredded
   sharp Cheddar cheese
1 cup finely chopped
   pepperoni
1 tablespoon olive oil

TIP

*Serve bread with an
oregano-infused dipping
oil. Combine 2 tablespoons
olive oil, ½ teaspoon black
pepper, 1 tablespoon
chopped green olives and
1 sprig fresh oregano. Let sit
several hours before serving
to blend flavors.*

1 Dissolve yeast in warm beer and milk in bowl of electric stand mixer. Attach dough hook to mixer. Stir in 2 cups all-purpose flour, rye flour, basil, sugar, salt and red pepper flakes until smooth. Stir in enough remaining all-purpose flour to form stiff dough. Add cheese and pepperoni. Knead on low 2 to 3 minutes or until smooth and elastic. Transfer to greased bowl; turning once to grease top. Cover and let rise in warm place until doubled, about 1 hour.

2 Punch dough down; divide in half. Shape into 2 (12-inch) loaves. Place on greased baking sheets. Cover; let rise in warm place until doubled again, about 45 minutes. Preheat oven to 350°F. Bake bread 30 to 35 minutes or until golden brown. Brush with oil.

CRUSTY PIZZA DOUGH

MAKES 4 SERVINGS

1 Dissolve yeast in warm water in bowl of electric stand mixer. Add 2½ cups flour, olive oil and salt. Attach dough hook. Turn mixer to low and mix 1 minute.

2 Continuing on low, add remaining flour, ½ cup at a time, and mix until dough clings to hook and cleans sides of bowl, about 2 minutes. Knead on low about 2 minutes longer.

3 Place dough in greased bowl, turning to grease top. Cover. Let rise in warm place, free from draft, about 1 hour, or until doubled in bulk. Punch dough down.

4 Preheat oven to 450°F. Brush 14-inch pizza pan with oil. Sprinkle with cornmeal. Press dough across bottom of pan, forming a collar around edge to hold toppings. Add toppings as desired. Bake 15 to 20 minutes.

1 package active dry yeast

1 cup warm water (105°F to 115°F)

2½ to 3½ cups all-purpose flour

2 teaspoons olive oil

½ teaspoon salt

1 tablespoon cornmeal

SOFT BEER PRETZELS

MAKES 12 PRETZELS

3¼ **cups all-purpose flour, divided**

1 **package rapid-rise active dry yeast**

1 **teaspoon salt**

6½ **cups water, divided**

⅔ **cup beer**

2 **tablespoons vegetable oil**

2 **tablespoons baking soda**

1 **egg, beaten**

Coarse salt

SHAPING PRETZELS

When shaping pretzels, make large exaggerated loops. Smaller loops will close when boiled.

1 Combine 3 cups flour, yeast and 1 teaspoon salt in bowl of electric stand mixer. Heat ½ cup water, beer and oil in small saucepan to 120°F. Attach dough hook to mixer. Mix beer mixture into flour mixture at low speed until moistened. Stir in enough remaining flour, 1 tablespoon at a time, to form soft dough. Knead on low 2 minutes or until dough is smooth and elastic. Cover and let rise in warm place 15 minutes.

2 Divide dough in half, then cut each half into 6 pieces. With lightly floured hands, roll each piece into 14-inch rope. (Cover remaining dough while working to prevent it from drying out.) Twist each rope into pretzel shape, pressing edges to seal. Place on greased baking sheets. Cover and let rise in warm place 15 minutes.

3 Preheat oven to 400°F. Bring 6 cups water to a boil in large saucepan; stir in baking soda. Working in batches, gently lower pretzels into boiling water; cook for 30 seconds, turning once. Using a slotted spoon, remove pretzels to wire rack coated with nonstick cooking spray.

4 Brush pretzels with egg and sprinkle with coarse salt. Bake 10 minutes or until golden brown. Cool on wire rack.

INDEX

COOKIES

YEAST BREADS

METRIC CONVERSION CHART

VOLUME MEASUREMENTS (dry)

$1/8$ teaspoon = 0.5 mL
$1/4$ teaspoon = 1 mL
$1/2$ teaspoon = 2 mL
$3/4$ teaspoon = 4 mL
1 teaspoon = 5 mL
1 tablespoon = 15 mL
2 tablespoons = 30 mL
$1/4$ cup = 60 mL
$1/3$ cup = 75 mL
$1/2$ cup = 125 mL
$2/3$ cup = 150 mL
$3/4$ cup = 175 mL
1 cup = 250 mL
2 cups = 1 pint = 500 mL
3 cups = 750 mL
4 cups = 1 quart = 1 L

VOLUME MEASUREMENTS (fluid)

1 fluid ounce (2 tablespoons) = 30 mL
4 fluid ounces ($1/2$ cup) = 125 mL
8 fluid ounces (1 cup) = 250 mL
12 fluid ounces ($1 1/2$ cups) = 375 mL
16 fluid ounces (2 cups) = 500 mL

WEIGHTS (mass)

$1/2$ ounce = 15 g
1 ounce = 30 g
3 ounces = 90 g
4 ounces = 120 g
8 ounces = 225 g
10 ounces = 285 g
12 ounces = 360 g
16 ounces = 1 pound = 450 g

DIMENSIONS

$1/16$ inch = 2 mm
$1/8$ inch = 3 mm
$1/4$ inch = 6 mm
$1/2$ inch = 1.5 cm
$3/4$ inch = 2 cm
1 inch = 2.5 cm

OVEN TEMPERATURES

250°F = 120°C
275°F = 140°C
300°F = 150°C
325°F = 160°C
350°F = 180°C
375°F = 190°C
400°F = 200°C
425°F = 220°C
450°F = 230°C

BAKING PAN SIZES

Utensil	Size in Inches/Quarts	Metric Volume	Size in Centimeters
Baking or Cake Pan (square or rectangular)	8×8×2	2 L	20×20×5
	9×9×2	2.5 L	23×23×5
	12×8×2	3 L	30×20×5
	13×9×2	3.5 L	33×23×5
Loaf Pan	8×4×3	1.5 L	20×10×7
	9×5×3	2 L	23×13×7
Round Layer Cake Pan	8×1½	1.2 L	20×4
	9×1½	1.5 L	23×4
Pie Plate	8×1¼	750 mL	20×3
	9×1¼	1 L	23×3
Baking Dish or Casserole	1 quart	1 L	—
	1½ quarts	1.5 L	—
	2 quarts	2 L	—